The Ultimate Coin Collecting Guide

4 Books in 1

A Comprehensive Numismatic Handbook for Building, Managing, and Profiting from Your Precious Coin Collection with Tips and Valuable Insights

Jonathan Morgan

Table of Contents

Book 1

Introduction

Welcome to the fascinating and story-rich world of coins! I am Jonathan Morgan, and I am honored to be your guide on this extraordinary journey through numismatics.

Coins are more than just pieces of metal. They are witnesses to the history, art, and culture of past and present civilizations. Each coin is a small work of art, a fragment of time that connects us to the past and opens a window to the wonders of the world. They are tools for exploring our shared history and for discovering the individual stories of those who created, owned, and exchanged them over the centuries.

In this book, I have tried to capture the beauty and importance of numismatics. It is an art that embraces aesthetics, history, culture, and passion, and through these pages, I will share with you my knowledge, experience, and passion for coins.

Who is the ideal reader for this book? Well, if you are an absolute beginner, curious to discover a new world, you are in the right place. If you are an experienced collector looking for insights and inspiration, you will find valuable information here. This book is designed for anyone who is fascinated by coins or who wants to begin an engaging journey in numismatics.

The structure of this book has been carefully designed to provide a logical progression from basic concepts to more advanced challenges. We will explore how to accurately identify, store, and value coins. You will learn how to build a collection that reflects your personal passion and interests. We will travel through numismatic cultures and eras from around the world, examining the most fascinating and significant coins.

Finally, we will explore the new frontiers of digital numismatics, including virtual coins and non-fungible tokens (NFTs), in an ever-evolving world.

So get ready for an exciting and educational experience as, together, we explore art, history, and culture through the fascination of coins. Numismatics is a fascinating journey and I am excited to share it with you. Are you ready? Then let's get started!

Chapter 1: Discovering Monetary Art

Coins: Milestones of Art and History

Coins are more than mere means of exchange; they are milestones that mark the course of human history. These small metal discs not only facilitated trade and transactions, but also told stories of mighty empires, ancient civilizations, and cultural revolutions. In this first subchapter, we will explore the central role of coins as works of art and witnesses to the past.

Coins as Artistic Expression: Since their origin, coins have been a means of artistic expression. Every civilization has used coins as a canvas to represent its culture, values, and identity. Coins have been decorated with images of gods and goddesses, charismatic leaders, national symbols, and depictions of significant historical events. Through these depictions, coins offer us a direct glimpse into the art of their time, allowing us to appreciate unique styles and details.

Coins as Historical Chronicles: Every coin tells a story. Legends and inscriptions engraved on coins often commemorate historical events or celebrate notable personalities. By carefully examining these inscriptions, we can reconstruct past events, from military conquests to political reforms, from cultural migrations to technological innovations. Coins are eyewitnesses to historical events and are often the only remaining records of certain periods.

Coins as Archaeological Treasures: Coins are not only works of art and tools of exchange; they are also archaeological treasures. They are often found during archaeological excavations, offering valuable information about ancient settlements and vanished civilizations. Each coin discovered is a piece of a larger puzzle that helps archaeologists better understand our shared history.

Coins as Mirrors of Civilizations: Finally, coins are mirrors of the civilizations that created them. Every detail, from the language used to the images chosen, reflects the culture and mentality of the people who minted them. Through the study of coins, we can immerse ourselves in past civilizations and discover their values, beliefs, and way of life.

In this chapter, we will further explore how coins have helped shape our understanding of art and history. We will discover how to recognize and appreciate the art engraved on them, as well as how coins have immortalized crucial moments in humanity. Are we ready to begin this fascinating journey of discovery of monetary art?

The Journey in Monetary Art: From Antiquity to Today

In our journey through monetary art, we will cross eras and civilizations, exploring how coins have reflected the evolution of human art and culture over the millennia.

Antiquity: The earliest coins, minted in civilizations such as ancient Lydia, Greece, and Rome, were often miniature works of art. They depicted gods and goddesses, mythological figures, national heroes, and cultural symbols. These coins were made with amazing artistry, considering the limited means available at the time.

Medieval Art: During the medieval period, coins became powerful tools for rulers. Often, coins featured portraits of the rulers or symbols of power. However, even during this period, artists and engravers sought to incorporate elements of beauty and creativity into their creations.

The Renaissance: The Renaissance was a time of renewed interest in art and culture. Coins reflected this change with anatomical details, realistic perspectives, and greater attention to aesthetics. Great artists such as Leonardo da Vinci and Donatello contributed to the art of coins.

The Modern Era: With the advent of advanced coinage technologies, modern coins can be incredibly detailed. In addition to portraits of political leaders and national figures, modern coins celebrate cultural, sporting, and ecological events. Contemporary coin art often embraces digital art and innovative design.

This journey through monetary art will take us across eras and cultures, examining how coins have been not only means of exchange but also artistic and cultural expressions. We will learn to recognize the artistic characteristics of different eras and how coins reflect the historical and cultural context in which they were minted. Ready to explore the fascinating world of coins through the lens of art and history? Let's continue our journey.

Coins As Miniature Works of Art

In the world of numismatics, coins are often considered true miniature works of art. In this subchapter, we will explore how coins have functioned as artistic media throughout history and continue to do so today.

Beauty in Monetary Art: Coins, though small, are extraordinary vehicles for art. Artists and engravers have used every inch of available space to create detailed and meaningful works of art. From intricate designs to realistic portraits, coins can surprise with their beauty.

Art in Detail: One of the most fascinating features of coins is their ability to include minute details. Skilled engravers have worked with specialized tools to create detailed images, often with stunning results. Even on small coins, you can see the fine lines of a portrait, the feathers of a bird, or the details of a historic building.

The Symbology of Monetary Art: Coins often not only represent aesthetic beauty, but also convey symbolic meanings. Whether through the use of mythological images, national symbols, or historical references, coins tell stories and convey cultural messages.

The Evolution of Monetary Art: Throughout history, monetary art has undergone several stages of evolution. From classical to modern art, coins have followed the artistic trends of their time. This evolution gives us a unique window into the history of art itself.

The power of coins as miniature works of art lies in their ability to capture attention and inspire curiosity. Each coin is a window into a different world, a bygone era, or a distant culture. Throughout this chapter, we will discover how art and numismatics are closely intertwined. We will learn to recognize the aesthetics of coins, interpret their symbols, and appreciate the skill of the artists who created them. The next step will take us into the "language" of coins, examining how images and symbols tell stories and convey deep meanings. We continue our journey into the fascinating world of coins.

Symbols and Engraved Stories: The Language of Coins

Coins, in addition to being miniature works of art, also carry a unique and fascinating language. In this subchapter, we will explore how coins communicate through engraved symbols and inscriptions, and how these elements help define their identity and meaning.

The Power of Symbols: Coins are filled with symbols, from mythological images to national emblems. Each symbol tells a story or expresses a value. You will learn to recognize these symbols and discover what they represent, thus revealing the stories hidden in the coins.

Inscriptions: In addition to images, coins often have inscriptions, which can be in different languages and alphabets. We will explore how to read and interpret these inscriptions, discovering important information about the coins, such as their place of issue, the date of minting, and the presiding leader.

History Told by Coins: Each coin is a small chapter in history. Through coins, you can follow the evolution of a civilization, its leaders, achievements, and cultural transformations. You will see how coins become silent witnesses to eras past.

The Fascination of Linguistic Numismatics: The interpretation of symbols and inscriptions on coins can be a fascinating challenge. But it is also an extraordinary way to immerse yourself in the history and culture of different regions of the world. You will discover how the language of coins can enrich your numismatic experience.

Throughout this subchapter, you will have the opportunity to decipher the secret language of coins. You will learn how to read symbols and interpret inscriptions, thus revealing the deeper meaning of the coins you collect or wish to collect. This is an essential step in your journey into numismatics, as it will allow you to fully appreciate the richness of coins as works of art and historical tools. We continue to explore the fascinating world of coins and their unique communication.

Monetary Art as a Mirror of Culture

Coins are not only pieces of metal with images and figures, but are also mirrors of the culture and society that created them. In this subchapter, we will examine how coins reflect the values, history, and identity of civilizations through time.

Historical and Cultural Context: Each coin is created in a specific context, and this is reflected in its design and symbols. We will explore how coins can tell the story of civilizations, from their triumphs to the challenges they faced.

The Depiction of Leaders and Heroes: Coins often depict rulers, military leaders, or national heroes. These images are not just portraits, but political and cultural messages that reflect the role of these figures within society.

Cultural and Religious Values: Coins can also reveal the cultural and religious values of a civilization. Religious symbols, deities, and rituals are often depicted on coins, offering a glimpse into the spirituality of past eras.

Technological and artistic innovations: The evolution of minting techniques and visual arts is reflected in coins. You will see how coins can become witnesses to the technological advancements and artistic trends of their time.

Examples of significant coins: Through specific examples, we will examine how different civilizations have used coins to express their cultural identity. From ancient Greek and Roman civilizations to Far Eastern cultures, we will explore a variety of significant coins.

Diagrams and Tables: As we explore this subchapter, we will use diagrams and tables to illustrate how coins can reflect cultural and historical changes over time. These visual tools will help you better understand the link between numismatics and culture.

Throughout this subchapter, you will discover how coins are more than just objects of material value. They are open windows into civilizations, cultures, and histories far back in time. You will learn to read between the lines of coins, revealing the historical and cultural context that made them unique. This will enable you to fully appreciate monetary art as a mirror of culture. Continue your fascinating journey into numismatics!

Chapter 2: The Collector's Tools – The Essential Kit

Your Basic Arsenal: Tools for Beginners

As you begin your journey into the world of coin collecting, it is essential to prepare yourself with the right tools. This subchapter will guide you through the process of creating your basic arsenal, giving you the information you need to get started in an effective and organized way.

Necessary to Begin

Although it may seem that coin collecting requires a sophisticated set of equipment, in reality, beginners can approach this hobby with a fairly simple set of tools. Here's what you need to get started:

Magnifying Glass: A good magnifying glass is essential. It will be your main tool for closely examining coins, revealing hidden details and small imperfections.

Numismatic Pliers: Numismatic pliers are designed to handle coins without damaging them. Be sure to buy a pair, preferably with plastic- or rubber-coated tips to avoid scratches.

Adequate Light: An adequate light source is essential for examining coins in detail. A daylight lamp or an adjustable LED light can be very helpful.

Digital Scale: An accurate digital scale will help you weigh coins accurately. This data is often important for coin evaluation.

Digital Caliper: A digital caliper measures the diameter of coins accurately. This tool is especially useful when it comes to identifying coins based on size.

Catalogs and Reference Books: As mentioned in the previous subchapter, a good collection of numismatic catalogs and reference books is essential. These will help you identify coins and understand their value.

Coin Case: A coin case will help you protect your coins from scratches and damage. Be sure to use PVC-free coin cases, as PVC can damage coins in the long run.

Where to Buy Tools

You can buy most numismatic tools at coin specialty stores or online. Be sure to do research and read reviews to find quality products. If you have the opportunity, talk to other coin collectors and ask for advice on which tools they prefer.

The Importance of Quality

The quality of the tools you choose is important. For example, a low-quality magnifying glass might distort the image of the coin instead of enhancing it. Investing in quality tools can make all the difference in your coin collecting hobby.

In this subchapter, we have reviewed the basic tools you need to begin your journey into coin collecting.

Magnifying Glass: The Collector's Eye

One of your best friends in the world of coin collecting will be a quality magnifying glass. This tool, simple at first glance, plays a vital role in coin inspection and identification. In this subchapter, we will explore the importance of the magnifying glass and how best to use it.

A Close and Personal Approach

Coins can be small, and some crucial details may escape your naked eye. The magnifying glass then becomes the collector's eye, allowing you to examine your coins in detail and revealing features that would otherwise go unnoticed.

Key Features of a Good Magnifying Glass

Not all magnifiers are the same, and there are different types. Here are some key features to look for when choosing a magnifier for your numismatic arsenal:

Adequate Magnification: Magnifiers are available with different levels of magnification. For most numismatic needs, a magnification between 5x and 10x is sufficient.

Optical Quality: Look for lenses with high-quality optics that do not distort the image and provide clear and sharp vision.

Illuminated Lens: Some magnifiers have built-in lights, which can be very useful for examining coins in low-light conditions.

Ergonomic Design: A magnifier with an ergonomic design is more comfortable to use for long periods and reduces eye fatigue.

Compactness and Portability: Choose a magnifier that is easy to carry with you on your visits to flea markets, numismatic exhibitions, or coin stores.

Affordable Price: It is not necessary to spend a fortune on a high-quality magnifier. Many affordable options offer excellent performance.

How to Use the Magnifying Glass

Using your magnifying glass correctly is essential to examine coins effectively. Here are some tips on how to do this:

Clean the Coin: Before examining a coin, make sure it is clean of any debris or impurities that might obstruct vision.

Adequate Lighting: Make sure you have a good source of light, natural or artificial, to illuminate the coin.

Proper Placement: Hold the magnifying glass at a distance of about 2.5–5 cm from the coin and move it slowly to examine all the details.

Coin Rotation: Rotate the coin as you examine it to see all sides and features.

Observe From Outer Band: Start examining the coin from the outer band and then move toward the center.

Make a List of Observations: Take note of important details, including scratches, hallmarks, and specific features of the coin.

Avoid Touching the Surface: When using the magnifying glass, try not to touch the surface of the coin with your fingers. Use numismatic tongs to handle it if necessary.

The magnifying glass will be a trusted tool during your journey into coin collecting, helping you discover hidden details, imperfections, and features that make each coin unique.

The Magic of the Numismatic Catalog

Numismatic catalogs are like fascinating maps that guide you through the vast world of coins. They are books full of valuable information and detailed tables and illustrations that allow collectors, from beginners to the most experienced, to explore a universe of coins from every corner of the world and every historical era. In this subchapter, let's dive into the magic of these essential tools for numismatic collecting.

The Numismatic Catalog: Your Essential Guide

A numismatic catalog is more than just a list of coins. It is a comprehensive guide covering a wide range of information regarding coins, from their history and provenance to their valuation and condition. These books are a crucial reference point for any serious collector.

Imagine having access to a virtual library of coins from around the world and from every historical era. A numismatic catalog offers you this possibility. You can browse through it to discover ancient coins from the Roman Empire, medieval European coins, colonial American coins, modern collectible coins, and much more. Each coin is accompanied by technical details, historical data, and, in many cases, appraisals that help you fully understand its value and significance.

Types of Numismatic Catalogs

Numismatic catalogs come in a variety of formats and specializations. You can find general catalogs that cover a wide range of coins from around the world, but there are also specialized catalogs that focus on coins from a specific region or a particular historical era. Your choice of catalog often depends on your interests and the type of collection you wish to build.

If you are a beginner, you might start with a generic catalog, which gives you a broad overview and helps you discover your preferences. If, on the other hand, you are already a fan of ancient Roman coins, you might opt for a specialized catalog that explores this category in detail.

How to Use a Numismatic Catalog

Now that you have a numismatic catalog in your hands, it is important to know how best to use it. These books are designed to be powerful research tools, but they can seem intimidating initially. Here are some guidelines on how to make the most of your catalog:

Navigating the Catalog: Numismatic catalogs are usually organized logically, with coins divided by region, era, or type. Take the time to familiarize yourself with the structure of the catalog so you can easily find the coins that interest you.

Interpreting the Information: Each entry in the catalog contains a wealth of information. Learn how to read and interpret this information, including technical details such as the diameter, weight, and metal of the coin, as well as historical data and curiosities.

Searching for Specific Coins: If you are looking for a particular coin, use the index or search function of the catalog. Enter the coin's name or other search criteria and follow the catalog's instructions to quickly find what you are looking for.

Advanced Searches: Once you become familiar with the catalog, you can perform more advanced searches. For example, you might search for all coins issued by a certain Roman emperor or a specific mint. Numismatic catalogs are designed to support detailed searches such as these.

Follow the Updates: Numismatic catalogs are often updated to reflect new discoveries and changes in the marketplace. Make sure you have the most recent version of the catalog or search online for updates and supplements.

A numismatic catalog is an invaluable resource for the coin collector. It is your passport to a numismatic adventure that spans time and space, allowing you to explore distant cultures and discover extraordinary coins.

The Digital World: Online Resources for Collectors

As technology has advanced, the world of coin collecting has opened up to new opportunities and online resources. This subchapter will guide you through the digital resources available to coin collectors and how to make the most of them.

Specialized Websites

There are numerous websites dedicated to coin collecting, each with its own features and resources. Some of these include:

Buy and Sell Sites: Platforms such as eBay, Heritage Auctions, and Stack's Bowers Galleries allow collectors to buy and sell coins from around the world.

Collectors' Forums: Online forums provide spaces to discuss, share experiences, and get advice from other collectors. Some well-known forums include CoinTalk and Collector's Universe.

Numismatic Companies Websites: Many numismatic companies have informative websites with online catalogs, coin guides, and appraisal services.

Research and Valuation Sites: Some sites offer research tools and value calculators to help you identify coins and estimate their value.

Numismatic Databases: Some websites offer access to extensive numismatic databases, with detailed information on coins from around the world.

Mobile Applications

Mobile apps have become increasingly popular among coin collectors. There are apps that allow you to catalog your collection, perform coin research, and even evaluate your inventory. Some of the most popular apps include PCGS CoinFacts, NGC Coin Explorer, and Coin Catalog.

Social Media

Social media is a great way to connect with other collectors, share your discoveries, and stay up to date on the latest numismatic news. Groups and pages dedicated to coin collecting on platforms such as Facebook can be very informative and interactive.

YouTube and Podcasts

Platforms such as YouTube host channels dedicated to coin collecting, where you can find videos on coin reviews, numismatic guides, and more. In addition, there are numismatic podcasts that offer audio content on various aspects of coin collecting.

Streaming Online Auctions

Some auction houses offer online streaming auctions, allowing you to participate in an auction from anywhere in the world. This is a unique opportunity to purchase rare and valuable coins.

Continuing Education

Digital technology provides opportunities for continuous learning. You can access guides, informative articles, webinars, and online seminars to enhance your numismatic knowledge. Some numismatic institutions offer online courses for collectors of all levels.

In this subchapter, we explored the digital world of coin collecting, highlighting the online resources and opportunities that are available to modern coin collectors.

Create Your Ideal Workspace

Creating a proper environment for your numismatic hobby is an essential step in maximizing your coin collecting experience. In this subchapter, we will explore how you can design and organize your ideal workspace that will allow you to catalog, examine, and store your coins with ease.

Dedicating a Physical Space

If you are fortunate enough to have extra space available, consider dedicating a specific room or area to your coin collection. Make sure this space is well lit, secure and free of moisture. Also, consider using shelves and cabinets to organize your coins and equipment.

Adequate Lighting

Light is crucial when it comes to examining and appreciating coins. Try to place your work area near a window or use adjustable LED lights for maximum control over brightness. Avoid direct sunlight, which can cause temperature changes and damage your coins.

Equipment and Tools

Your workspace should be well equipped with the essential tools for coin collecting. These may include magnifying glasses of different powers, tweezers to handle coins gently, cotton gloves to avoid fingerprints, and calipers to measure coin sizes.

Organization

Organization is the key to maintaining an accurate inventory of your collection. You can use numismatic albums, folders, or coin-specific crates to keep track of your coins in an orderly manner. Label each coin with clear information, such as date of acquisition, provenance, and special characteristics.

Digital Cataloging

Consider using numismatic cataloging software to keep track of your collection digitally. These programs allow you to enter detailed information about each coin, including historical data, condition, and value. Many numismatic apps also offer scanning capabilities to record images of your coins.

Security

The security of your coins is of paramount importance. If your collection is of significant value, consider installing a security system in your work area or in the room where you store your coins. Safety deposit boxes in a bank are also an option to consider for the rarest and most valuable coins.

Regular Maintenance

Finally, remember to perform regular maintenance of your workspace. Clean and organize your environment periodically to avoid dust accumulation or clutter. Keeping your workspace in excellent condition will ensure that you can fully enjoy your numismatic hobby.

In this subchapter, you learned the importance of creating a proper working environment for coin collecting. From lighting to organization, every detail will help improve your experience.

Chapter 3: Deciphering the Mystery of Coins – A Guide to Recognition

The Keys to Identification: Reverse, Obverse, and Edge

Accurate coin identification is the foundation of numismatic collecting. In this subchapter, we will examine the three main areas of a coin that provide important information for identifying it: the obverse, reverse, and edge.

The Observe: The Face of the Coin

The obverse is the front side of the coin, often called the "face." It usually features the profile of a person or a representative effigy. The obverse may include such elements as the name of the sovereign, the date of issue, national symbols, and other significant details. This part of the coin is crucial in determining its origin and historical period.

The Reverse: The Heart of Iconography

The reverse is the back side of the coin, commonly known as the "crown." This section usually features significant symbols, images, or cultural representations. It may depict objects, historical scenes, mythological figures, or other elements emblematic of the issuing country. By carefully analyzing the reverse side, you can gain valuable information about the historical and cultural context of the coin.

The Edge: Unexpected Details

The edge of a coin can also provide important information. It can be smooth, knurled, grooved, or have specific engravings. Some coins have text or symbol engravings on the edge, offering additional clues to their origin or destination. Careful examination of the edge can reveal valuable details that contribute to accurate identification.

Identification Considerations

When identifying a coin, look carefully at both the obverse and reverse, paying attention to the details of the images, artistic styles, and inscriptions. Check for dates, names, or distinctive marks. In the case of the obverse, pay attention to any special engravings or features.

Use numismatic guides, online catalogs, and specialized resources to help you with identification. Guides can offer detailed information on different coins, including images and descriptions that can be compared with your coin.

Learning to recognize and correctly interpret details of the obverse, reverse, and edge of coins will help you build an accurate and thorough collection.

Science or Art? The Visual Analysis of Coins

In the world of numismatics, visual analysis is a fundamental skill for collectors. In this subchapter, we will explore how to look closely at coins and how visual analysis can reveal crucial details about their authenticity, condition, and value.

The Art of Observing: From Surface to Detail

Looking at a coin is not just a matter of looking, but of seeing. Visual analysis involves the close examination of every aspect of the coin, from images to text, from patina to hallmarks. For example, ancient coins may show signs of wear and tear that tell of their history and circulation through time.

Authenticity: Recognizing Copies and Counterfeits

Visual analysis is a powerful tool for detecting counterfeit or copy coins. By carefully studying image details and comparing them with authentic sources, it is possible to identify significant differences that indicate a possible counterfeit. This is especially important when purchasing coins from unverified sources.

State of Preservation: From Day One to Circulation

Visual analysis can reveal much about the state of preservation of a coin. Often, well-preserved coins show sharp details, while those that have circulated for many years may show signs of wear and abrasion. Numismatic experts use a condition rating scale to grade coins according to their degree of wear.

Aesthetic Value: The Appreciation of Monetary Art

In addition to technical aspects, visual analysis allows us to appreciate the art present in coins. Coins often feature finely engraved details, artistic symbols, and unique styles that reflect the era and culture in which they were minted. Visual analysis allows you to admire these miniature works of art and understand their historical and cultural significance.

Tools for Visual Analysis

To perform an accurate visual analysis, it is helpful to use tools such as magnifying glasses and daylight lamps. These tools can reveal hidden details and help you assess the condition of coins.

From Magnificence to Minute: Analysis of Characteristics

In the fascinating world of numismatics, analyzing the characteristics of coins is a crucial step in fully grasping their historical and artistic value. In this subchapter, we will dive into the physical details of coins, carefully examining their size, weight, design, and special features that make each coin a true work of art.

Size and Weight: The Physicality of Coins

The size and weight of a coin are key data for its identification and evaluation. These physical aspects provide valuable information about the coin itself and its historical placement. You will learn how to accurately measure the size and weight of your coins, comparing them to numismatic specifications to determine the authenticity and grading of coins.

Design and Symbols: The Heart of Monetary Art

The design of a coin is its artistic calling card. Each coin is a small masterpiece, with images, figures, and symbols that tell stories of past eras. In this chapter, you will delve into monetary art, learning to decipher the meaning of the designs engraved on coins. You will discover how these visual elements reflect the culture, politics, and society of the period in which the coins were minted.

Detecting Anomalies: Distinguishing Signs and Variants

In analyzing features, it is critical to be attentive to details. Coins may have distinctive marks, design variations, or unique features that make them special. You will learn how to spot these anomalies and assess their importance in the numismatic context. Each small variation could reveal fascinating details about the coin's history.

Legends and Inscriptions: The Language of Coins

Coins often bear engraved legends and inscriptions, which add a layer of textual meaning to their visual beauty. In this chapter, you will learn how to read and interpret these legends and inscriptions, discovering how they contribute to the narrative of the coins themselves. Engraved words can reveal crucial information about the provenance, historical period, and authority that minted the coin.

Technical Characteristics: Materials and Coining Processes

Feature analysis also includes an understanding of the materials used to mint coins and the minting processes adopted in various historical periods. You will be able to recognize the types of metals, alloys, and minting techniques used over the centuries, gaining in-depth knowledge that can influence the value and history of the coins you collect.

Feature analysis is a fundamental pillar of becoming a competent numismatist.

Guide to Reading Legends and Inscriptions

A significant part of the appeal of coins lies in the legends and inscriptions engraved on them. These texts tell stories, document historical events, and reveal details that can transform a coin from a simple object to a fascinating piece of history. Learning to read and interpret these legends is essential for a collector or numismatics enthusiast. Here is a detailed guide on how to do so:

1. Identification of Alphabet and Language: The first step in deciphering a legend is to identify the alphabet and language used. Coins may have text written in a variety of languages, from the Latin alphabet to Greek, Arabic, Chinese, or even ancient scripts such as Egyptian hieroglyphics. Recognizing the alphabet will help you determine the geographical area and historical period of issue.

2. Translation and Meaning: Once you have identified the language, proceed with translation. If you are not an expert linguist, you may need to consult specialized resources, books, or experts. Try to find out what the legends say: they may contain names of sovereigns, titles, places of issue, or even political slogans. These details can reveal a lot about the coin.

3. Dating: Many legends include dates or references to specific events. These can be essential for accurately dating the coin and placing it in a historical context. For example, a date might correspond to the year of the ruler's coronation or a military victory.

4. Motto or Slogan: Some coins include mottos or slogans that reflect the ideals or beliefs of the era. These elements can add depth to the meaning of the coin and offer additional historical perspective.

5. Variants and Errors: As you examine the legends, pay attention to variants or minting errors. These details can make a coin particularly interesting to collectors. For example, a legend may have a different spelling or typo, making that coin unique.

6. Historical References: Legends may refer to relevant events, historical figures, or places. Doing research on related history can further enrich your understanding of the coin and the context in which it was issued.

The ability to decipher legends and inscriptions on coins will enable you to discover fascinating stories and gain a deeper understanding of numismatic heritage. Don't be in a hurry, as sometimes translation can be complex, but with practice, you will become increasingly proficient in reading and interpreting these valuable historical annotations.

When Touch Makes a Difference: Material and Weight

In addition to visual characteristics and legends, the material and weight of a coin can provide important clues to its authenticity, value, and history. This sub-\chapter focuses on how to evaluate the material and weight of coins and what to look for when collecting or investing in coins.

1. Material of the Coin: The material from which a coin is minted can vary greatly. Coins can be made of precious metals such as gold, silver, or platinum, or less precious metals such as copper or nickel. Identifying the material is crucial because it greatly affects the value of the coin. For example, gold and silver coins often have significantly higher intrinsic value than coins made of less precious metals.

2. Authenticity Verification: The material of a coin can help verify its authenticity. For example, gold or silver coins are often counterfeit, so it is important to perform authenticity tests when buying precious coins. These tests may involve checking the weight, diameter, and sound of the coin.

3. Weight of the Coin: Weight is a key indicator of a coin's authenticity and value. The weight specifications of a coin are often detailed in numismatic sources. Verify that the weight of the coin matches the specifications in the catalog or reference source. Significant deviations from the standard weight may be a sign of counterfeiting or excessive wear.

4. Common Materials vs. Precious Materials: Consider whether you want to collect coins made of precious materials or coins made of more common metals. Precious metal coins usually retain their intrinsic value over time but can be expensive to acquire. Base metal coins may be a more affordable choice but may not have the same appreciation potential.

5. Storage and Cleaning: The material of a coin can also influence how it should be stored and cleaned. For example, silver coins can develop the patina of oxidation over time, which can be considered part of their appeal. However, some coins made of less noble metals may require special precautions to prevent deterioration.

6. Diversification: Consider how coin material fits into your overall collection or investment strategy. Diversification into different types of material can help balance the risk and growth opportunity of your collection.

Evaluating the material and weight of coins is an essential part of the decision-making process for numismatic collectors and investors. Understanding these characteristics will help you make informed decisions and build a solid numismatic collection or portfolio.

Chapter 4: The Treasure in the Drawer – Keeping Coins with Care

Secrets of Preservation: Protecting Your Heritage

Proper storage of your coins is essential to preserving their integrity, value, and appearance over time. In this chapter, we will explore the secrets of coin storage, from recommended materials and methods for protection to avoiding deterioration and safe cleaning.

1. Protect from External Threats: Coins can be vulnerable to many external threats, including moisture,

oxidation, polluted air, and weathering. To protect your coins, consider using sealed containers specifically for numismatic storage. Clear plastic containers or specially designed capsules are great for protecting coins from weathering and contamination.

2. Materials and Methods of Storage: Use high-quality storage materials. Avoid touching the coins with your fingers, as contact can transfer oils and dirt to the surface. Use cotton or nylon gloves when handling coins. Coins should be handled over a soft surface, such as a clean cloth, to avoid damage if dropped.

3. Protect from Patina: Some collectors appreciate patina, the surface oxidation that can develop on antique coins. However, if you wish to keep your coins patina free, try to avoid moisture and polluted air. Using airtight containers and dehydrators can help prevent patina formation.

4. Safe Cleaning of Coins: Cleaning coins is a delicate operation and should be done only in extreme cases. Generally, it is preferable not to clean coins, as many methods can damage them irreparably. If you feel that a coin needs to be cleaned, consult a numismatic expert for professional advice.

5. Long-Term Storage: If you want to preserve your coins for future generations, think about how you are storing them. Well-preserved coins should be stored in a cool, dry, dark place. Avoid exposing them to direct sunlight or extreme temperature changes.

6. Insurance: Consider the option of insuring your numismatic collection. Specialized insurance policies for coins can offer peace of mind in case of loss, theft, or damage.

Coin preservation requires care and attention, but it is an investment of time and resources that can help maintain the value and appearance of your coins over the years. Pay attention to detail and follow best storage practices to ensure the longevity of your numismatic collection.

Materials and Methods: A Guide to Coin Preservation

Preservation of coins is essential to maintain their value and beauty over time. In this subchapter, we will explore the essential materials and methods for the proper preservation of your numismatic coins.

1. Clean Hands and Gloves: Before touching any coins, make sure your hands are clean and dry. Using white cotton gloves will help prevent the accumulation of oils and debris.

2. Protective Cases: Store your coins in protective cases specifically designed for numismatic coins. There are several options, including clear plastic cases or acrylic cases. Make sure they are free of materials that can damage coins, such as PVC.

3. Storage Sheets: The storage sheets are useful for organizing and protecting your coins. You can place coins in the transparent compartments of the sheets to avoid direct contact with each other.

4. Avoid Excessive Cleaning: Excessive cleaning of coins can damage them irreparably and reduce their value. In general, avoid cleaning coins unless absolutely necessary, and if you do, consult a professional.

5. Controlling the Environment: Store your coins in an environment with controlled temperature and humidity. Avoid extreme fluctuations in these conditions, as they can cause damage.

6. Periodic Maintenance: From time to time, check your coins for signs of deterioration or oxidation. If there are any problems, act promptly to prevent further damage.

7. Adequate Storage: When not showing your coins, store them in a safe place, protected from the elements, such as a safe. Make sure the safe is anchored securely.

Proper storage of your numismatic coins is essential to preserving their value and beauty over time. By following these guidelines, you can enjoy your collection for years to come and pass it on to future generations in pristine condition.

Invisible Enemies: How to Avoid Deterioration

The world of coins is fascinating, but it hides some unseen enemies that can irreparably damage your precious collections. In this subchapter, we will explore the main enemies of coins and how to avoid them.

1. Oxygen and Moisture: Oxygen and moisture can cause oxidation on coins, creating stains or color changes. To avoid this, store your coins in a low-humidity environment and use airtight containers or cases that prevent air access.

2. Contact with Acidic Materials: Coins in contact with acidic materials may suffer corrosion. Make sure the cases or storage sheets in which they are placed are acid free.

3. Inadequate Handling: Touching coins with fingers can transfer oils and debris, causing staining and dullness. Use white cotton gloves or handle coins only by the edges.

4. Excessive Light: Prolonged exposure to direct sunlight can fade the colors of coins and cause fading. Store your coins in a dark place or use a light with low UV emission in case of exposure.

5. Cross-Contamination: Keep coins of different materials or alloys separate, as contact between different metals can cause corrosion.

6. Inappropriate Cleaning: Cleaning coins aggressively or using abrasive cleaners can cause permanent damage. If you must clean a coin, consult a numismatic expert for proper instructions.

7. Long-Term Storage: If you intend to store coins for a long time, use high-quality storage materials and check conditions regularly to make sure everything is in order.

8. Smoke and Pollution: Smoke and air pollution can cause discoloration and damage to coins. Keep an environment free of smoke and chemical pollution.

9. Excessive Handling: Avoid handling coins excessively or dropping them, as they may get scratched or dented.

Recognizing these invisible enemies and taking preventive measures to protect your coins is critical to keeping them in optimal condition. Investing in proper storage will allow you to preserve the value and beauty of your numismatic coins over time.

Safe Coin Cleaning: Restoring Original Beauty

Coins, over time, can accumulate dirt, residue, and oxidation that affect their aesthetics and value. However, cleaning coins is a delicate art that must be performed with great care to avoid irreversible damage. In this subchapter, we will examine how to safely clean coins and restore their original beauty.

1. Avoid Using Harsh Cleaners: Both household cleaners and abrasives can damage coins. Absolutely avoid using chemicals such as bleach, ammonia, or vinegar, which can cause corrosion or fading.

2. Mechanical Cleaning: In many cases, mechanical cleaning of coins should be avoided, as it can cause scratches or abrasions. However, in some cases where coins are heavily oxidized, an experienced numismatist could use specific tools to remove the oxide layer without damaging the coin surface.

3. Distilled Water and Mild Soap: The safest technique for cleaning coins involves the use of distilled water and a mild soap. Soak the coin in distilled water for a few minutes and then rub it gently with your fingers or a soft-bristled brush. Dry the coin carefully to prevent staining.

4. Ultrasound: Some collectors use ultrasonic devices, which use high-frequency sound waves to remove dirt from coins. This technique requires care and must be performed by experienced people.

5. Patina: Some collectors prefer to maintain the natural patina of coins, which can add aesthetic value. Patina is the layer of oxidation that forms on the surface of the coin over time. Cleaning can remove it, so consider whether it is really necessary to clean the coin.

6. Advice from a Professional: If you have coins of great value or interest, it is always advisable to consult an experienced numismatist before proceeding with cleaning. They can provide personalized advice based on the specific coin and your needs.

Always remember to be extremely cautious when deciding to clean a coin. A mistake in cleaning can greatly reduce its value. In general, cleaning should be an option of last resort, and it is often preferable to preserve the coin's original patina.

Long-Term Preservation: Your Collection for Future Generations

Proper storage of your coins is essential to ensure that they retain their value and beauty over time and can be passed down to future generations. In this subchapter, we will explore best practices for the long-term preservation of your numismatic collection.

1. Controlled Environments: Store your coins in a controlled environment with stable temperature and relative humidity. Avoid exposure to direct sunlight and change the air periodically to prevent moisture buildup.

2. Use High-Quality Containers: Buy high-quality numismatic containers, such as PVC-free plastic cases or sealed air-capsule containers. These will protect your coins from outside contaminants and scratches.

3. Safe Handling: Handle coins with cotton or nylon gloves to avoid transmission of oils and acids from the skin. Keep coins by the edges to avoid touching surfaces.

4. Labeling: Carefully label each coin with key information such as date, mint, and grade. This will help keep track of your collection and simplify future upgrades or sales.

5. Avoid Over-Cleaning and Cleaning: As mentioned above, avoid over-cleaning coins, as it may compromise the patina. If necessary, consult a professional for cleaning.

6. Regular Inventory: Take regular inventory of your collection to ensure that all coins are in place and in optimal condition.

7. Documentation and Insurance: Keep complete records of your collection, including photographic records and coin appreciations. Insure your collection to protect it from unforeseen events such as theft or natural disasters.

8. Involve the Family: If you intend to pass your collection on to future generations, involve your family members in the care and appreciation of your coins. This can help preserve your numismatic heritage.

9. Periodic Maintenance: Inspect your coins periodically for signs of deterioration or corrosion. Coins should be stored in high-quality containers, but may require maintenance over time.

10. Consult a Professional: If you have coins of great value or historical importance, consult an experienced numismatist regularly to evaluate your preservation and maintenance options.

Long-term preservation is critical to protecting the value and beauty of your coins over generations. By following these guidelines, you will be able to keep your numismatic collection in excellent condition for the future.

Book 2

Chapter 5: Start Your Collection – Choose the Right Coins for You

The Initial Choice: Coins—Where to Start?

In this subchapter, we will explore the crucial first step for any aspiring coin collector: deciding where to start your collection. You will discover several paths you can take and learn how to evaluate which one is best for you.

The Vast World of Coins

Coins have been minted all over the world for centuries, which means you have a wide range of options to choose from. We will discuss the different categories of coins, from ancient to contemporary, and help you figure out which might be your first choice.

Thematic Collecting: Follow Your Passion

Thematic collecting is one of the most fascinating ways to start your own collection. We will help you discover how to focus on a topic of interest to you, such as Roman coins or commemorative coins, creating a collection rich in personal meaning.

Dream Coins: Hunting for Rare and Precious Coins

If you are attracted to the challenge and search for treasure, we will discuss collecting rare and valuable coins. You will learn how to identify the rarest and most desirable coins and how to participate in specialized auctions and markets.

Things to Avoid: Questionable Coins and Purchases

In the world of coin collecting, there are some pitfalls to avoid. We will share tips on how to recognize counterfeit coins or scams and how to make informed purchases.

Where to Find Your Coins: Markets, Exhibitions, and More

Finally, we will guide you through the different sources from which you can acquire your coins, which include markets, exhibitions, specialty stores, and even buying online. You will be able to plan your first step in your exciting numismatic adventure.

After exploring this subchapter, you will have a clear understanding of how to start your own coin collection. You will discover the different options available and be able to make informed decisions about the direction you want to go in the world of numismatic collecting.

Thematic Collecting: Follow Your Passion

Thematic collecting is a fascinating way to begin your adventure in numismatics. In this approach, collectors focus on coins that represent a specific theme or personal interest. This can add deep meaning to your collection and make the experience even more engaging. Here are some key considerations:

Choose Your Theme: The first thing to do is to select the theme of your collection. It can be anything from ancient Roman coins to U.S. quarters issued in commemoration of national parks. Choose something that you are passionate about and inspired by.

Deepen Your Knowledge: Once you have chosen your theme, it is important to deepen your knowledge about it. Study the history, culture, and events related to your theme. This knowledge will help you make informed decisions when looking for new coins to add to your collection.

Research and Purchase: Thematic collecting will give you clear direction when looking for coins to purchase. You can attend numismatic fairs, explore online coin stores, or contact other collectors with similar interests. Remember to watch out for suspicious buyers and always check coins for authenticity.

Create a Narrative: As your collection grows, consider creating a narrative around your theme. You can write detailed stories or descriptions for each coin, explaining why it is important to you and how it fits into the context of your theme.

Share Your Passion: Thematic collecting can be a lonely experience, but it doesn't have to be. Participate in online or local communities of collectors who share your interest. This will connect you with people who understand your passion and may even suggest new additions to your collection.

Thematic collecting is an exciting way to start collecting coins, and it offers endless opportunities to explore the world of numismatics through the filter of your personal interest. So if you have a passion or a theme you are passionate about, why not start your thematic collection today?

Dream Coins: Hunting for Rare and Precious Coins

One of the greatest thrills of coin collecting is the hunt for rare and valuable coins. These numismatic treasures can be the beating heart of your collection and present a fascinating challenge. Here's how to hunt for rare and precious coins:

Identify Coins of Interest: Before you begin your hunt, you need to know which coins interest you most. This could include ancient coins, coins with minting errors, rare coins from a specific nation or era, and more. Clearly identify your collecting goals.

Research and Study: Hunting for rare coins requires a lot of research and study. You must familiarize yourself with the characteristics of the coins you wish to find, learn about their variants, and understand how to recognize an authentic coin. Specialized books, numismatic magazines, and online resources can help you at this stage.

Attend Auctions: Numismatic auctions are a great place to find rare and valuable coins. Attending an auction can be an exciting experience, and you may have a chance to win a desired coin. Be sure to set a budget and do your research in advance.

Explore Markets and Shops: In addition to auctions, visit local numismatic markets and look for stores specializing in coins. Some dealers may have rare coins in their inventory. Your network of numismatic contacts can also be a valuable source for your research.

Make Use of Advanced Technology: Today, technology can help you in your hunt for rare coins. You can use tools such as metal detectors or coin identification apps. These tools can increase your chances of finding hidden treasures.

BE PATIENT AND CONSISTENT: Hunting for rare coins requires patience and perseverance. Don't expect to find your treasure right away. Keep looking, learn from the experts, and stay passionate. The gratification of finding a rare coin is unique.

Have Your Discoveries Appraised: When you think you have found a rare coin, have its authenticity and condition appraised by experts. This will help you determine the value of the coin and ensure that you have a genuine treasure in your hands.

The hunt for rare coins is an engaging adventure that can enrich your numismatic collection and knowledge. Remember to enjoy the journey and share your discoveries with other collectors.

Things to Avoid: Questionable Coins and Purchases

In the world of numismatic collecting, there are some pitfalls and situations to avoid to ensure that your experience is rewarding and profitable. Here are some things to keep in mind and avoid:

Impulsive Purchases: Resisting the impulse to buy a coin just because it looks interesting is crucial. Before making a purchase, study the coin, research information about its authenticity and value, and consider whether it fits your collection and goals.

Lack of Research: One of the biggest challenges for collectors is lack of research. Do not underestimate the importance of studying and learning as much as possible about the coins you are interested in. Lack of knowledge can lead to costly mistakes.

Neglecting Authenticity: The authenticity of coins is crucial. Buy only from reputable sources and, when necessary, verify the authenticity of the coin through experts or authentication services. Counterfeit or forged coins can be costly and detrimental to your collection.

Ignoring the State of Preservation: The state of preservation of a coin has a significant impact on its value. Do not ignore this aspect. Learn to assess the state of preservation and watch out for damaged or improperly cleaned coins.

Making Purchases Without a Budget: Before you start collecting coins, set a realistic budget. This will help you avoid spending more than you can afford and keep control of your finances.

Lack of Adequate Conservation: Storage of coins is essential to preserve their condition. Do not neglect this aspect. Invest in high-quality storage cases and materials to protect your coins from wear and deterioration.

Buying from Untrustworthy Sellers: Choose reputable sellers and sources when buying coins. Research the seller and look for reviews or recommendations from other collectors. Avoid sellers who seem unclear or unprofessional.

Ignoring Market Trends: The coin market is constantly changing. Staying informed about trends and price fluctuations is essential, especially if you are investing in coins. Don't neglect monitoring the market.

Not Sharing the Interest: Collecting can be a lonely experience if not shared with others. Join collectors' groups, online forums, or local clubs to share your passion, learn from others, and expand your network of contacts.

Giving Up Too Soon: The hunt for rare coins can take time and patience. Don't give up too soon if you haven't yet found the treasure you seek. Keep looking and learn from your experiences.

By avoiding these common pitfalls, you can make your coin collecting experience more rewarding and successful. Remember that collecting is an ongoing learning journey, and each coin tells a unique story.

Where to Find Your Coins: Markets, Exhibitions, and More

Once you have decided which coins you want to collect, you need to know where to find them. There are several options available for buying numismatic coins, each with its own advantages and considerations.

Numismatic Markets: Numismatic markets are events where collectors and vendors gather to exchange coins. These events can be local or national and offer a wide range of coins to examine and purchase. It is a great way to see coins in person and shop from reputable sellers.

Numismatic Auctions: Auctions are a popular option for purchasing rare and valuable coins. Auction houses auction off coins of high value and rarity, often with a detailed description and valuation.

Attending an auction can be exciting, but it is important to set a budget and refrain from exceeding it.

Numismatic Dealers: Dealers specializing in numismatic coins are reliable sources for buying coins. They choose their coins based on authenticity and quality criteria and can provide expert advice. Research reputable dealers and check their reviews.

Numismatic Exhibitions: Numismatic exhibitions are temporary events where collectors and dealers display their coins. You can examine a wide range of coins and shop directly from vendors. Check to see if there are any exhibitions scheduled in your area.

Online Stores: There are numerous online stores specializing in numismatic coins. You can peruse their offerings from the comfort of your own home, and you will often find a wide selection of coins to choose from. However, be careful to select reputable online stores with clear return policies.

Private Purchases: Some collectors prefer to make purchases directly from other collectors through private sales. This can be done through online ads or through connections in the numismatic community. Be sure to research and evaluate coins carefully before making a private purchase.

Numismatic Fairs: Numismatic fairs are larger and longer-lasting events than numismatic markets. They can host numerous vendors and offer a wide selection of coins. Numismatic fairs can be excellent opportunities to meet other collectors and gain new knowledge.

Collectors' Groups: Participating in local collectors' groups or online forums is a way to connect with other numismatic enthusiasts. Often, members of these groups sell or trade coins with each other.

Banks and Exchange Offices: In some cases, you may find interesting numismatic coins at banks or exchange offices. Although less common, you may make some interesting discoveries.

When choosing where to buy your coins, consider your experience and level of knowledge. If you are a novice, you may want to start with reputable dealers or attend local numismatic exhibitions to learn and build your collection gradually. Also, always do your research before making a purchase and set a budget to avoid overspending.

Chapter 6: The Secret Value of Coins – A Guide to Valuation

Unraveling the Mystery of Monetary Value

In the world of numismatics, one of the most fascinating and complex aspects is coin valuation. Every coin has a value, but determining that value can be an art in itself. In this first subchapter, we will explore how to unravel the mystery of monetary value and the factors that influence what a coin is worth in the marketplace.

Understanding Numismatic Valuation

Numismatic valuation is the process of determining how much a coin is worth based on a number of factors. These factors can vary greatly from coin to coin and can include:

Conservation Condition: One of the most important factors in evaluating a coin is its condition. Coins in better condition and without obvious signs of wear are generally more valuable. Collectors use specific grading scales, such as the Sheldon scale, to assess the state of preservation of a coin.

Rarity: Rarity is another crucial factor in determining the value of a coin. Rare coins, often related to minting errors or limited production, may be worth considerably more than more common coins.

Year of Minting: The year in which a coin was minted can affect its value. Some years may be rarer or have historical significance, which makes coins from that year more desirable to collectors.

Mint of Coinage: The mint that struck a coin can have an impact on its value. Some mints are more renowned than others for their quality and precision in coin production.

Unique Factors: Some coins have unique factors that make them especially desirable. These may include minting errors, variations, or special features that distinguish them from other coins of the same type.

Assessment Tools

To help you evaluate a coin, there are several tools and resources available:

Numismatic Catalogs: Catalogs such as the "Red Book" in the United States or the "Krause Standard Catalog of World Coins" list and evaluate a wide range of coins. They are excellent resources for collectors.

Numismatic Auctions: Auctions can provide a current valuation of coins similar to those you own or are looking to buy. You can see at what price similar coins have sold recently.

Applications and Websites: There are many applications and websites dedicated to numismatics that offer valuation tools based on parameters such as condition, year, and mint of mintage.

Expert Advice: When you have a high-value or complex coin to appraise, it may be wise to seek the advice of numismatic experts. These professionals have experience in appraisal and can offer an accurate estimate of your coin's value.

Avoiding Scams and Fraud

In the world of coin collecting, there are also scams and frauds to consider. Before buying or selling a coin of significant value, research the seller or seek expert advice to ensure its authenticity.

Key Factors: What Determines the Value of a Coin?

Now that we have addressed the importance of coin valuation, it is time to look at the key factors that influence the value of a coin. Understanding these factors will help you more accurately value your coins and make informed decisions in the world of numismatics.

State of Preservation

The condition of a coin is one of the most critical factors in determining its value. Coins are rated on a condition scale ranging from "Never Circled" to "Heavily Worn." This scale is often called the Sheldon scale, named after its creator, numismatist William Sheldon.

Major categories include:

Never Circulated (Mint State): These coins are in mint condition and have never circulated. They are graded from MS-60 (the lowest) to MS-70 (the highest).

Circulated: These coins have signs of wear due to circulation, such as scratches, finger marks, and wear on the images. They are graded according to the degree of wear.

Heavily Worn: These coins have suffered a considerable degree of wear and tear and may be severely damaged.

Rarity

Rarity is another critical factor in the evaluation of a coin. Rare coins, often related to minting errors or limited production, may be worth much more than more common coins of the same type. Some examples of rare coins include obvious minting errors, such as double struck coins or reverse struck coins.

Supply and Demand

The basic law of economics, supply and demand, also applies to coins. If a coin is particularly in demand by collectors but is available in limited quantities, its value may rise considerably. Conversely, if a coin is readily available and demand is low, its value may be modest.

History and Meaning

The value of a coin can also be influenced by its history and significance. Coins with an interesting history or related to important historical events may be more desirable to collectors and therefore more valuable.

Mint of Coin

The mint of minting, or the place where a coin was produced, can influence its value. Coins minted in mints that are prestigious or famous for their quality are often more highly valued.

Artistic Aspects and Design

The artistic appearance and design of a coin can influence its value. Coins with attractive designs, carefully engraved miniature works of art, or elaborate details may be more valuable because of their aesthetic value.

Valuation Tools: How to Calculate Monetary Value

The art of numismatic valuation is a crucial aspect for coin collectors and investors. Each coin has its own unique value, which can vary based on a number of factors. In this subchapter, we will delve into the valuation methodologies and tools used by numismatists to accurately determine the value of a coin.

Valuation Methodologies: Various valuation methodologies exist, and experienced collectors often combine them to obtain an accurate estimate. We will look at how to use the auction-based approach, comparison with specialized numismatic guides, condition analysis, and other techniques to determine the value of a coin. You will learn how these methodologies can vary depending on the type and age of the coin.

State of Preservation: A crucial factor in the valuation of a coin is its state of preservation. The overall condition of a coin can greatly influence its value. We will explore the different conservation grades, from "Brilliant Uncirculated" to the most worn coins, and how these classifications can make a difference in prices. You will also learn how to spot signs of wear or damage that could reduce a coin's value.

Market Choices: The numismatic market is dynamic and can be influenced by a number of factors, including demand, supply, and market trends. We will look at how market choices can impact the value of coins. Knowing the market environment can help you make informed decisions about buying and selling. We will also examine how to identify trending coins that may increase in value over time.

Technology and Numismatic Appraisal: The advent of technology has made advanced appraisal tools more accessible. We will discuss how specialized software and apps can simplify the coin appraisal process. These tools can offer detailed information on market quotes, price changes, and even the historicity of coins.

Case Studies: To put the valuation methodologies into practice, we will look at some case studies of specific coins. Each case will give us the opportunity to apply the knowledge gained in this subchapter and see how numismatic valuation principles translate into practice. You will be able to better understand how to appraise real coins and make decisions based on these appraisals.

Numismatic appraisal is an essential skill for anyone involved in the world of coins, whether they are avid collectors or investors. With a solid understanding of valuation methodologies and the factors that influence the value of coins, you will be able to manage your collection in a more informed way and make better decisions about purchases and sales. Continue exploring this subchapter to hone your numismatic appraisal skills.

Price Right: How to Avoid Depreciation and Overestimation

Determining the value of a coin is not only a matter of knowing the factors that influence the price, but also of avoiding common pitfalls such as devaluations and overestimates. In this subchapter, we will examine how to value coins fairly, avoiding both devaluations and overestimates, to ensure informed buying and selling decisions.

Balance of Supply and Demand: One of the main reasons why coins can be overvalued or devalued is a lack of understanding of the relationship between supply and demand. We will explore how the limited supply of a coin, combined with strong demand from collectors, can increase its value. At the same time, we will discover how an oversupply or lack of interest can lead to devaluation.

Examples of Overvalued Coins: To better understand the dangers of overvaluation, we will examine historical cases of coins that have been overvalued in the market. These examples will help us identify warning signs when it comes to valuing coins. We will learn to be skeptical when prices seem too high relative to real demand.

Risks of Devaluation: On the other hand, we will see how devaluation of a currency can cause it to lose value. This can happen when a currency is overvalued initially, but then its value stabilizes or declines due to lack of interest. We will learn how to avoid buying coins that may be prone to devaluation.

Trend Analysis: One way to avoid both overvaluation and devaluation is to analyze market trends. We will explore how to monitor price changes over time and identify coins that show steady growth or increasing demand. This knowledge will enable you to make smarter choices in your numismatic portfolio.

Fair Trading: Finally, we will discuss how to negotiate fairly when buying or selling coins. You will learn how to recognize situations where you can get a better price or where it is fair to accept a particular quote. Your negotiation skills can greatly influence the success of your transactions.

Avoiding overpricing or devaluing coins is critical to ensuring that your collection maintains its value and continues to grow over time. With a clear understanding of supply and demand balance principles, historical examples, and trading strategies, you will be able to make more informed decisions in the world of coins. Continue exploring this subchapter to hone your numismatic appraisal skills.

Monitoring the Market: Keeping the Assessment Updated

As we further explore the world of numismatic valuations, it is essential to understand that the value of coins can fluctuate over time. This can be influenced by a number of factors, including collector interest, market trends, and historical events. In this subchapter, we will examine how to monitor the market to keep your coin valuation up to date and make informed decisions about purchases and sales.

Market Fluctuations: We will first understand that the coin market is dynamic, with valuations that can change in response to a variety of factors. We will explore how economic events, changes in collector preferences, and new coin discoveries can influence market fluctuations.

Sources of Information: To keep your coin appraisal up to date, you need to be aware of reliable sources of information. We will review several resources, including numismatic publications, specialized websites, and numismatic auctions. You will learn how to use these sources to monitor changes in value in the coin world.

Factors Influencing Value: We will discuss factors that can influence the value of a coin over time. These factors include rarity, preservation, market demand, silver and gold fluctuations, and collecting trends. Understanding how these elements intersect will help you better value your coins.

Valuation Tools: We will explore the tools and techniques used to assess the value of coins in today's market. These tools may include appraisal software, up-to-date numismatic guides, and advice from experts in the field. You will learn about the resources available to you for obtaining accurate estimates.

Keeping a Record: A recommended practice for every collector is to keep an accurate record of their coins. We will discuss how to record important information, including current coin valuations, conditions, and provenances. A well-maintained record will help you track the value of your collection over time.

Keeping the valuation of your coins up to date is critical to making informed decisions about their future. By exploring the factors that influence the market and taking advantage of reliable sources of information, you will be able to accurately assess the value of your coins and ensure that your collection maintains or increases in value over time.

Chapter 7: Uncovering Counterfeit Coins – How to Recognize Them and Protect Your Collection

Introduction to Counterfeit Coins

The integrity of your numismatic collection is of utmost importance. The sad reality is that the market for counterfeit coins is constantly growing. Counterfeit coins can range from simple imitations of old and rare coins to sophisticated copies of valuable coins designed to fool even experienced collectors. In this chapter, you will learn how to recognize counterfeit coins and protect your valuable numismatic heritage.

Why Recognizing Counterfeit Coins Is Important

Numismatics is a fascinating hobby that can also be a significant investment. The value of many coins can increase significantly over time, attracting the interest of collectors and investors. This interest has led to the rise of counterfeit coins on the market, and it is essential to know how to recognize them. Buying or trading counterfeit coins can lead to significant financial losses, damage a collector's reputation, and compromise the validity of a collection. Therefore, it is crucial to learn how to distinguish between genuine and counterfeit coins.

The Consequences of Counterfeit Coins

Counterfeit coins have a number of harmful effects:

Financial Losses: Buying counterfeit coins can lead to significant financial losses, especially if they are investment coins.

Risk of Buying Stolen Material: Counterfeit coins often circulate among criminals, so there is a risk of buying stolen material.

Reputation Damage: A collector who purchases counterfeit coins may see his or her reputation damaged among the numismatic community.

Impact on the Collection: Counterfeit coins can infiltrate your collections and affect their overall authenticity.

Chapter Objectives

In this chapter, we will explore the common characteristics of counterfeit coins, useful tools for recognizing them, commonly counterfeit coins, and actions to take to protect your collection. It will be a comprehensive guide on how to become an expert in recognizing counterfeit coins and defending your numismatic heritage.

Common Characteristics of Counterfeit Coins

To become proficient in recognizing counterfeit coins, it is essential to understand the common characteristics that distinguish these imitations from genuine ones. Counterfeit coins can vary greatly in quality, but some recurring characteristics include:

Missing Details: Counterfeit coins often have less defined details than their genuine counterparts. Check facial features, inscription, and decorative elements.

Incorrect Material: Some counterfeit coins may be made of different metals than genuine ones. For example, a fake gold coin might be made of a less precious metal.

Inconsistent Weight and Size: The weight and size of a coin are critical criteria. Counterfeit coins may not have the correct size or weight.

Non-Uniform Surfaces: Check the surface of the coin for obvious imperfections or defects, such as air bubbles, scratches, or melt marks.

Erroneous or Absent Quality Marks: Many genuine coins carry quality marks or specific mint marks. Counterfeit copies may have errors or lack these marks.

Abnormalities in Your Stray: Some counterfeit coins may show signs of erosion or oxidation that are not typical of genuine coins.

Price Too Tempting: Beware of offers that are too good to be true. If the price of a coin seems incredibly tempting, it could be a red flag.

Uncertain Mint Signatures or Mint Marks: Carefully examine mint signatures and mint marks. Abnormalities or irregularities are often signs of a counterfeit coin.

Error in Dates or Legends: Check the dates and legends on the coin for any errors or discrepancies.

Coarse Handiwork: Counterfeit coins often display a lower level of craftsmanship than genuine coins.

Lack of Adequate Documentation: Always check the documentation, history, and authenticity of the coin before making a purchase.

It is important to note that counterfeit coins can vary in quality and accuracy of reproduction. Some imitations may look strikingly authentic, while others may show obvious signs of counterfeiting. Later in this chapter, we will delve into specific tools and techniques to detect these characteristics and identify counterfeit coins.

Remember that recognizing counterfeit coins requires practice and constant study. It is not a skill acquired overnight, but your commitment will protect you from costly mistakes.

Tools for Recognizing Counterfeit Coins: Identifying Inauthenticity with Accuracy

Recognizing counterfeit coins requires not only the use of the right tools, but also a thorough understanding of how to use them. In this subchapter, I will guide you through the precise use of these tools so that you can recognize counterfeit coins with confidence.

Magnifying Glass: A good-quality magnifying glass is a crucial ally. Make a complete assessment of the coins, looking closely at details such as the consistency of engravings and the sharpness of images. Check for small signs of counterfeiting, such as drawn marks or unsharp engravings.

Precision Scale: Use a precision scale to carefully weigh coins. Authentic coins should match specific standard weights. If you notice even a small discrepancy in weight, it could be a sign of counterfeiting.

Vernier Caliper: This tool accurately measures the size of coins. Make sure you have a good understanding of the standard size of authentic coins and use the caliper to verify the size of coins in your collection.

Magnetometer: The magnetometer detects magnetic materials in coins. Gently pass the magnetometer over the coins to detect traces of magnetic materials that should not be present in genuine coins.

Thickness Gauge: Use the thickness gauge to accurately measure the thickness of coins. Authentic coins should have a specific thickness. Any discrepancy could be a sign of counterfeiting.

Examination of Engraved and Relief Features: Look closely at the incuse (carved on the inside) and relief (raised) features of coins. Authentic coins show consistent details and sharp engravings.

To help you put these techniques into practice, I will provide examples of famous coins that have been subject to counterfeiting throughout history. Understanding these tools and applying this knowledge will enable you to successfully protect your collection from counterfeit coins. Remember, constant practice and gaining experience are critical to becoming an expert in authentic coin recognition.

Common Counterfeit Coins: Knowing the Threats to Your Collection

An essential part of recognizing counterfeit coins is understanding which coins are often counterfeit. Here, I will guide you through some of the most commonly counterfeit coins, enabling you to be more aware of threats to your collection:

Morgan Silver Dollar: This popular U.S. coin has been widely counterfeited. Features to check include the layout of the engravings, the presence of mint errors, and the consistency of the numerals. Use the magnifying glass to inspect details, such as the eagle's feathers or Morgan's hair.

Krugerrand: The Krugerrand is a famous gold investment and is therefore a target for counterfeiters. Counterfeits can range from the use of non-pure gold alloys to engraving errors.

Double Eagle: This U.S. gold coin has been subject to numerous counterfeits. Look carefully at the texture of the detail, including the edges, and use the precision scale for weight.

Canadian Gold Maple Leaf: These coins are highly counterfeit. Check the engravings, weight, and diameter accurately. Make sure the edge is free of irregularities.

American Gold Liberty: These gold coins have been counterfeited using non-pure alloys. Check the weight, size, and overall appearance to confirm authenticity.

Antique Coins: Antique coins from around the world can be targets for counterfeiting. Counterfeits can range from simple to sophisticated. Use the magnetometer and other recognition techniques to protect your collection.

Rare Foreign Coins: Rare coins from other nations are often counterfeited to exploit their rarity. Buy from reputable sources and carefully check the specifics of the coin.

By keeping these common coins prone to counterfeiting in mind, you will be more aware of potential threats to your collection. Be sure to examine these coins carefully when adding them to your collection and use the tools described in the previous subchapter to confirm their authenticity.

Actions to Take to Protect Your Collection: Defend Yourself from Counterfeits

Now that you know the common characteristics of counterfeit coins and have learned how to use recognition tools, it is time to take concrete steps to protect your collection. Here are some actions you can take:

Buy from Reliable Sources: A good starting point for avoiding counterfeit coins is to buy from reliable sources, such as long-standing numismatic dealers, recognized auction houses, and lending institutions. Be cautious when buying from unfamiliar sellers online or at trade shows.

Verify Authenticity: Before purchasing a coin, use the recognition tools and inspection techniques described above. Request certifications of authenticity from recognized sources.

Keep Detailed Documentation: Keep a detailed record of each coin in your collection. This can include pictures, source documents, and any pertinent information.

Insurance: Insure your collection against counterfeiting and other losses. This will provide you with a financial safety net in case of problems.

Choose Proper Storage: Store your coins in a controlled environment, away from harmful weathering. Proper storage reduces the risk of damage or counterfeiting.

Periodic Updates: Keep up to date on new counterfeiting techniques and developments in the world of numismatics. Attend conferences and seminars, read trade journals, and stay informed.

Share with Experts: When in doubt about the authenticity of a coin, feel free to share it with recognized numismatic experts. The numismatic community is an important resource for verifying authenticity.

Continue Education: Invest time in continuing education about recognizing counterfeit coins. Knowing your collection thoroughly makes you more resistant to counterfeits.

Join Numismatic Associations: Join local or national numismatic associations. These organizations offer resources and support to collectors.

Remember that prevention is key. Not only will these actions protect your collection, but they will also make your numismatic journey richer and safer. Continue to improve your skills and strengthen your awareness of counterfeit coins to ensure an authentic and valuable collection.

Chapter 8: Cataloging Your Coin Collection – A Step-by-Step Guide

The Magic of Cataloging: Turning Coins into Historical Stories

Welcome to the wonderful world of numismatic cataloging. In this first subchapter, we will explore the magic of bringing your coin collection to life through cataloging. You will understand how this process can transform an assortment of metal pieces into a rich collection of historical stories, making you the keeper of a cultural and personal heritage.

The Power of Catalogued Coins

Imagine owning coins from distant eras or remote regions of the world. Each coin is a fragment of history, a link in the mosaic of humanity. Cataloging allows you to unlock the potential of these coins. Each piece becomes a story to be told.

Preserving Historical Memory

Cataloging your coins allows you to keep your historical memory alive. You can connect each coin to an era, a place, and even a specific event. These connections reveal not only the history of the coins but also the history of humanity.

Creating a Personal Bond

Cataloging is not just an academic endeavor. It is an opportunity to make a personal connection to your collection. Every time you document a coin, you contribute to the history of your personal collection. Every time you tell the story of a coin, you contribute to your personal story as a collector.

Your Complete Guide

This subchapter will give you a taste of the power of cataloging. It will be a journey through history, art, and culture, all through your coins. You will learn how to bring each coin to life and create a personal archive that will nurture your passion and interest in numismatics.

Welcome to the magic of cataloging—the first step in turning your coins into unique historical stories. Continue exploring this chapter to find out how to begin this exciting journey.

Before You Begin: Preparing for a Successful Cataloging Trip

Before you fully immerse yourself in the world of numismatic cataloging, it is essential to prepare for a successful journey. In this subchapter, we will guide you through the preparations necessary to ensure that your cataloging experience is smooth and highly rewarding.

Cataloger's Tools

A good cataloger is only as good as the tools he or she has at his or her disposal. Before you start, make sure you have everything you need. These tools include a magnifying glass, tweezers, numismatic gloves (to avoid direct contact with coins), precision scales, and calibrated rulers. Each tool has a specific role in ensuring accurate cataloging.

Adequate Working Space

A well-organized work environment is essential. Make sure you have enough space to examine and catalog coins comfortably. Good lighting is crucial, so invest in adequate lighting or take advantage of natural light. Keep your workspace free of distractions and interruptions.

Organization System

Developing an effective organization system is essential. You can use folders, file cabinets, or specialized numismatic cataloging software. The important thing is that you can easily keep track of information about each coin, including year, country of origin, value, and history.

Preliminary Studies

Become familiar with numismatic terms and conventions. Study catalogs and numismatic reference resources to understand how the information is organized. This will help you catalog your coins consistently and accurately.

Photographic Documentation

Photographic documentation is critical. Photograph each coin from different angles, ensuring that details are clearly visible. These images can be useful for future reference and for sharing your collection with other collectors.

Enthusiasts and Experts

Consider getting involved with the numismatic community. Participating in online forums, collectors' groups, or local meetings will allow you to share experiences, get advice, and even access expert knowledge. Sharing with other collectors can greatly enrich your cataloging experience.

Before you begin your cataloging journey, by following these preparations, you will be well positioned for successful cataloging. Get ready for a deep dive into the world of your coins, where every detail and story will have the power to surprise you. Continue exploring this chapter to delve further into the cataloging process and advanced techniques.

Cataloging for Beginners

In this subchapter, we will guide you through the essential first steps to cataloging your coins. Even if you are a beginner, don't worry: cataloging can be a rewarding and relatively simple process, especially if you follow this step-by-step guide.

Basic Identification

The first step in cataloging is to identify your coins. This includes country of origin, date of minting, coin type, and mint. Use resources such as books, online catalogs, or, if possible, expert advice to obtain this information.

Detailed Visual Examination

A detailed visual examination is essential. Carefully inspect each coin with a magnifying glass for details such as engravings, legends, and overall condition. This step will help you better evaluate your coins.

Photographic Documentation

Another important practice is to document your coins photographically. Take clear, well-lit photos of each coin, capturing the most important details. These photos can serve as a useful reference for you and, if you ever decide to sell or insure your collection, for others.

Detailed Registration

Prepare a detailed record for each coin. In addition to the basic information, note any special features, any defects, and your personal evaluation.

Protection and Preservation

Finally, make sure that each coin is stored properly. Use high-quality numismatic cases to avoid physical damage and oxidation.

Once you have completed these steps, you will be ready to catalog your coins more accurately and document your collection professionally.

Coins from Around the World

In this chapter, we will delve into the cataloging of coins from different parts of the world. The numismatic world is vast and diverse, and each region has its own rich monetary history. Here is how you can approach cataloging coins from around the world:

Select a Region of Interest

Begin by selecting a specific region or country to explore. This can be based on your existing collection or a personal interest. For example, you might focus on ancient Roman coins or explore colonial American coins. The choice is yours.

In-Depth Research

Once you have chosen your region, begin your research. Use specialized books, numismatic catalogs, and online resources to discover specific coins and gain knowledge about their history, value, and characteristics.

Sort Coins

Organize coins by criteria such as date, minting mint, composition, and face value. You can use index cards or spreadsheets to keep track of each coin and related information.

Detailed Labeling

Carefully label each coin with a unique reference number linked to your registry. Be sure to include all relevant information, such as the name of the sovereign or issuing entity, date of minting, and any other significant features.

Detailed Description

In addition to labels, create a detailed description for each coin in your catalog. This description should cover physical appearance, major features, any distinguishing marks, and your personal rating.

Organized Catalog

Keep your catalog organized and up to date. You may want to use specialized coin cataloging software that makes it easier to manage information about a large collection.

Cataloging coins from around the world is an exciting experience that will allow you to immerse yourself in the cultures and histories of different regions. Be sure to be thorough and systematic in your cataloging to maximize the value and usefulness of your numismatic collection.

Advanced Cataloging

Advanced cataloging is an essential step for any coin collector who aims to create a well-organized and documented collection. This step allows you to go beyond simply recording coins and create a comprehensive, richly detailed catalog. Here is how you can perform advanced cataloging:

State of Preservation

In the advanced catalog, you must pay special attention to the state of preservation of each coin. Use the standard grading system, such as theSheldon scale, to assign each coin an accurate state of preservation. This will greatly influence the overall value of your collection.

Quality Photographs

In addition to describing your coins in detail, take high-quality photographs of each coin. This is essential for documentation and display of your collection. You can use a good-quality digital camera or a smartphone with good resolution. Be sure to clearly capture the details of the coin, such as the obverse and reverse, as well as any special features.

Detailed Register

Update your record with more and more detailed information. In addition to basic information such as the sovereign's name, date of minting, and mint of production, you may want to record additional details such as weight, diameter, rim type, and any special markings on the coin. This additional information will be invaluable both to you and to possible buyers or subsequent custodians of your collection.

Evaluation and Certification

If you intend to sell or insure your collection, consider professional appraisal and certification. These services are offered by recognized bodies and can add authority to your collection. A certified appraisal can also help you determine the current value of your coins accurately.

Adequate Archiving

With advanced cataloging, it is even more important to store coins properly. Make sure each coin is protected from damage and changes in environmental conditions. Use high-quality storage cases and keep your collection in a suitable environment.

Advanced cataloging is a step that requires time and dedication, but the benefits in terms of managing and enhancing your coin collection will be substantial. Your collection will become a valuable resource and potentially a legacy for future generations.

Cataloging Software and Tools:

In an increasingly digitized world, there are many resources and software dedicated to cataloging coins. Using these platforms can greatly simplify the process of organizing and managing your collection. Here's how you can take advantage of cataloging software and tools:

Choice of Software:

The first step is to select coin cataloging software that meets your needs. There are various options available on the market, some free and some paid. Before committing to a specific software, consider the following aspects:

Ease of use: Make sure the software is intuitive and you can use it with ease. A friendly user interface makes the cataloging experience more enjoyable.

Features: Check to see if the software offers advanced features such as the ability to enter specific details about the state of preservation, attach high-quality photos, and manage a complete inventory.

Support for Grading System: If you plan to grade your coins according to a standard of condition, make sure the software supports this system.

Compatibility: Check whether the software is compatible with your operating system and whether it offers a mobile or cloud-based version for mobile access.

Data Entry:

Once you have chosen the software, start entering data on your collection. This process takes time, but it will allow you to create a detailed and easily manageable catalog. Be sure to include the following information:

Basic data: Name of sovereign, date of minting, mint, country of issue, and other essential details.

Conservation status: Uses the standard rating system to assign a conservation status to each coin.

Description: Give an accurate description of the features, design, and any special markings on the coin.

Images: Upload high-quality images of the coin, capturing details on both obverse and reverse.

Management and Updates:

Once your collection has been cataloged, it is important to keep it up to date. Add new purchases and edit information as you discover new details about your coins. Maintaining an accurate catalog is critical to the long-term management of your collection.

Data Backup:

Finally, don't forget to make regular backups of your catalog data. Choose a secure method to save the information, such as cloud storage or an external hard drive. Backups ensure that the data in your collection is protected from accidental loss.

Using cataloging software and tools can transform the management of your coin collection, simplifying the process and giving you a detailed view of your coins. Choose the software that best suits your needs and start creating a comprehensive catalog.

Methods of Organization

Coin cataloging is an essential step in managing a numismatic collection, but the real key to a well-organized collection lies in adopting effective methods. Here are some common approaches you can follow:

Organization by Country or Region:

This is one of the most intuitive methods and is especially suitable if you collect coins from different parts of the world. You can divide your collection into sections devoted to each country or region, creating a clear structure.

Chronological Order:

Another option is to organize coins by year of minting. This is especially useful if you want to follow the evolution of coins over time or if you focus on a specific historical era.

Thematic Groups:

A theme-based approach can be fascinating. For example, you can create sections devoted to coins with portraits of sovereigns or similar designs, or even coins commemorating historical events.

Classification by Mint:

If you are particularly interested in the different mints that minted the coins, you can organize your collection according to this criterion. This requires a thorough knowledge of numismatic mints.

Order of Evaluation:

A value-based approach is useful if you collect coins for investment purposes. You can organize coins according to their market value, keeping the most valuable ones in a separate section.

Cataloging System:

Following a standard cataloging scheme can simplify management. For example, you can use the Krause-Mishler cataloging system for world coins.

Combination of Methods:

Often, collectors combine several methods to organize their collection in more detail. For example, you can organize coins by country and within each section, divide them chronologically.

Labeling and Filing:

In addition to a method of organization, be sure to label your coins with clear details. Use protective bags or containers and create labels with relevant information, such as country, year, and condition.

Digital Catalog:

Using cataloging software allows you to create comprehensive cross-referenced digital catalogs. These tools simplify organization and allow you to quickly find the coins you want.

Monitoring Acquisitions:

Keep an accurate record of the coins you buy or sell, along with information about the purchase, price, and seller's details. This helps you keep track of the value of your collection and its growth over time.

Choose the approach or combination of methods that best suits your needs and your collection. Good organization not only simplifies coin management, but also allows you to fully appreciate the beauty and history of each piece.

Photography and Documentation

Accurate photography and documentation are key aspects of coin cataloging. These steps help you keep a complete record of your collection and provide important information for valuing and selling coins. Here's what you should consider:

Quality Photographic Tools:

To obtain clear and detailed images of your coins, it is essential to use good-quality photographic tools. A digital camera with good resolution and a macro lens will be an invaluable tool.

Adequate Lighting:

Light is critical to achieving high quality images. Use diffused light or avoid direct lighting to avoid glare. Natural light or dimmable LED lights can be good options.

Backgrounds and Supports:

Use neutral backgrounds, such as plexiglass panels or white or gray background fabrics. An adjustable camera stand will help keep the frame stable.

Camera Settings:

Learn how to use your camera's manual settings to control aperture, shutter speed, and ISO sensitivity. This will enable you to capture details optimally.

Adequate framing:

Be sure to frame the coin so that it is centered and perfectly in focus. Take multiple photos from different angles to capture all the details.

Detailed Documentation:

Next to each photographed coin, keep a record with detailed information. This information includes country, year of minting, mint, condition, and any distinguishing features.

Cataloging and Archiving Software:

Use numismatic cataloging software that allows images to be associated with coin information. This simplifies collection management.

Numbered Labels:

Assign a unique number to each coin and use numbered labels to link physical coins to images and information in the catalog.

Backup Images:

Be sure to regularly back up images to external or cloud devices. This precaution prevents the loss of valuable data.

Registry Maintenance:

Update the coin register regularly with new acquisitions or relevant details. Keeping the register accurate is critical to monitoring the value of the collection over time.

Photography and documentation are investments in the future of your collection. A well-documented and well-photographed collection is easier to value, sell, and share with other numismatic enthusiasts. Be sure to devote time and effort to these crucial steps.

Your Complete Guide to Cataloging

In this section, I will provide you with a detailed and comprehensive guide to cataloging coins. Follow these steps to create a complete and organized catalog for your numismatic collection.

Step 1: Prepare the Necessary Tools

Before you start, make sure you have all the necessary tools:

Coins: Your numismatic collection.

Camera: A good-quality digital camera with a macro lens.

Adequate Light: Make sure you have diffused light or adjustable lighting.

Camera Stand: An adjustable stand to keep the frame stable.

Backgrounds: Choose neutral backgrounds, such as plexiglass panels or white or gray fabrics.

Computer: For storage and management of images.

Cataloging Software: Choose numismatic cataloging software that fits your needs.

Step 2: Organize the Collection

Before you start cataloging, physically organize your coins. You can do this by country, historical period, mint, or any criteria you prefer. Make sure each coin is clean and free of debris.

Step 3: Coin Photography

Frame each coin so that it is centered and perfectly in focus.

Take multiple photos from different angles to capture all the details.

Make sure the images are of high quality and well lit.

Associate each image with the corresponding coin in the cataloging software.

Step 4: Documentation

Record detailed information for each coin, including country, year of minting, mint, condition, and other relevant features.

Cataloging software can assigns a unique number to each coin and uses numbered labels to link physical coins to images and information in the catalog.

Step 5: Use Cataloging Software

Use numismatic cataloging software to create your digital catalog. This simplifies management and research within your collection.

Upload images and information for each coin into the software.

Regularly update the catalog with new acquisitions or relevant details.

Step 6: Back Up and Archive

Be sure to regularly back up your images and catalog to external devices or cloud storage services.

Keep the coin register up to date and organized.

Step 7: Continuous Maintenance

Update the coin register with new acquisitions, changes in condition, or changes in value.

Continue to improve your photography skills to get better and better images.

Step 8: Share Your Collection

With a comprehensive and well-documented catalog, you will be ready to share your collection with other numismatic enthusiasts or, if you wish, to consider sale options.

Step 9: Continuous Learning

Coin cataloging takes time and practice. Continue to learn and improve your skills over time.

This comprehensive guide will help you create a numismatic catalog that will enable you to manage, enhance, and share your collection effectively.

Chapter 9: Coins from Around the World – Journey into Numismatic Cultures

Global Treasures: A Search in Coins from Different Regions

Welcome to Chapter 9, where we will embark on a journey through numismatic cultures from around the world. We will begin this exploratory journey by focusing on the concept of "global treasures," coins from different regions of the planet that offer us a fascinating glimpse into history and cultural diversity.

1. Coins from Every Corner of the World: Numismatics is an open window into different cultures and historical periods. In this subchapter, we will examine a selection of representative coins from various parts of the globe, each with its own unique story to tell.

2. Coins as Witnesses to the Past: Coins have functioned as vehicles of communication and testimony to the respective periods in which they were minted. By observing these coins, we can discover much about the politics, culture, traditions, and external influences of the societies that created them.

3. Ancient Civilizations: From ancient Egypt to the Roman Empire, from imperial India to ancient China, we will explore the coins that were in circulation in these great civilizations and how they helped define their identity and history.

4. Representative Coin Examples: During this journey, we will present some specific coins as examples, including Greek drachmas, Roman aureas, Indian rupees, and Venetian zecchini. We will learn about their symbols, cultural meanings, and historical significance.

5. The Universality of Coins: Despite cultural differences, coins share a universal language of value. We

will explore how different civilizations met the challenge of creating monetary systems and what role these currencies played in the growth and development of their societies.

6. Numismatic Art: In addition to economic value, many of these coins are true miniature works of art. We will examine the aesthetics of coins from different cultures, highlighting how art has often been used to represent symbols of power and identity.

This subchapter is an immersion in the cultural and historical diversity represented by coins from around the world. Each of these coins is a small treasure that tells a story, and through our numismatic journey, we hope you will gain a new perspective on the richness of global history.

Journey Through Time: Historic and Contemporary Coins

In the second subchapter of our journey through the numismatic cultures of the world, we will dive into the temporal dimension of coins. We will explore historical and contemporary coins from different eras, offering a more complete picture of the diversity and evolution of cultures through numismatics.

1. Coins as Chroniclers of Time: Coins are not only means of exchange, but true chroniclers of the eras in which they were minted. We will look at how coins have changed over the centuries, reflecting the economic, technological, and cultural developments of their respective eras.

2. Ancient Coins: We will begin our journey by going back in time, examining ancient coins that have stood the test of centuries. From ancient Greek coins with their mythological depictions to Roman coins with portraits of emperors, we will explore the world of coins that have shaped history.

3. Medieval Coins: Through medieval coins, we will discover the dark and enlightened periods of Europe and other parts of the world. Medieval coins often reflect the importance of religion and the kings and dynasties that ruled.

4. Colonial and New World Coins: We will also examine coins minted during the era of exploration and colonialism, highlighting how these coins marked the contact between different cultures and societies.

5. Modern Coins: We will then move to the modern period, examining the coins of recent centuries and their connections to historical events, wars, and revolutions. We will discover how modern numismatics reflects the evolution of industrialized and globalized societies.

6. Historical and Collector Value: We will not overlook the importance of the historical and collector value of coins. Some ancient or rare coins are highly valued by collectors, and understanding their history is essential to appreciating their value.

This subchapter will take us on a journey through historical eras, from ancient civilizations to modern eras. Each coin tells a unique story, and through our exploratory journey, we hope you will gain a new understanding of the evolution of cultures and societies around the world.

Where Art Meets History: Iconic Coins of Ancient Cultures

In this third subchapter, we will take an exciting journey through the iconic coins of ancient cultures. Each coin is a piece of art and a historical record in miniature. We will explore different eras and cultures through the following coins:

1. Greek and Roman Coins: Ancient Greek coins often feature wonderful designs celebrating Greek mythology. We can find figures such as Athena, Zeus, and Heracles, as well as intricate artistic details. On the other hand, Roman coins are fascinating for their portraits of emperors and empresses, offering insight into Roman politics and society.

2. Coins of Ancient Egypt: Egyptian coins are an encyclopedia of symbols and culture. Many of them depict pharaohs, deities, and sacred objects such as the sarcophagus. By examining these coins, we can discover the religion, history, and art of ancient Egypt.

3. Coins of Ancient China: Chinese coins feature Chinese characters and cultural symbols. These coins represent a bridge between the art, language, and history of ancient China. Some of them date back to dynasties, such as the Tang Dynasty and the Qing Dynasty.

4. Coins of the Byzantine Empire: Byzantine coins are renowned for their intricate iconography. They often depict the reigning emperor and religious figures such as Jesus Christ and the Virgin Mary. These coins are important not only numismatically, but also for the religious and political history of the Byzantine Empire.

5. Coins of Pre-Columbian Cultures: The pre-Columbian cultures of the Americas, such as the Aztecs and Incas, left behind unique coins. These coins show images of deities, sacred animals, and cultural symbols. They are valuable records of these civilizations before European contact.

In this subchapter, through detailed descriptions and images, we explore these fascinating iconic coins, offering a captivating journey through the art and history of ancient cultures. Each coin is a piece of a larger puzzle, an open window into a world that would otherwise be lost in the maze of time.

Representative Coins: National Symbols and Pride

This fourth subchapter will take us on a journey through representative coins, those that encapsulate the symbolism and pride of nations and cultures. These coins are often the most recognizable and admired in the world. We will look at some of the most valuable and fascinating:

1. The American Bald Eagle (U.S.): The one-dollar coin of the United States, commonly called the "Morgan Dollar," is famous for the image of the bald eagle on the front. This coin symbolizes American pride and independence.

2. The Maple Leaf (Canada): The one-ounce Canadian maple gold coin is famous for its simple and

refined design with a maple leaf. This coin represents Canada and its natural wealth.

3. The Chinese Panda (China): The Chinese Golden Panda is known for its ever-changing designs depicting pandas. Each year features a different panda, symbolizing this magnificent animal native to China.

4. The Kijang Emas Dragonfly (Malaysia): This Malaysian coin depicts a golden dragonfly, a symbol of freedom and prosperity. It is one of the most sought-after gold coins by collectors in Asia.

5. The African Elephant (Somalia): The Somali silver coin features an elephant, a symbolic animal for Africa. Each year, the design changes, representing different species of African elephants.

6. The Year of the Dragon Coin (Australia): Australia issues Year of the Dragon coins to celebrate Chinese astrology. These coins are sought after for their artistic design and the connection between Australian and Chinese cultures.

7. Canadian Polar Bear (Canada): Canada celebrates its affinity with the Arctic through Polar Bear coins. These coins represent the importance of nature and conservation.

8. The British Lion (United Kingdom): The British lion is a symbol of strength and majesty. The United Kingdom has issued several coins with depictions of lions to celebrate its history and culture.

The Importance of Representative Coins: These coins represent not only national symbols but also often incorporate unique cultural and historical elements. They are beloved by collectors for their intrinsic value and their ability to tell the story and identity of a nation.

Exotic Collector Coins: Hunting for Unique Treasures

In this fifth subchapter, we will dive into the world of exotic collectible coins, those that defy convention and capture the imagination of collectors around the world. We will explore some of the most valuable and extraordinary coins, each with its own fascinating history:

1. The Silver Kookaburra Coin (Australia): The kookaburra is a bird native to Australia, known for its distinctive song. This silver coin often features a portrait of a kookaburra and changes its design every year, making it highly coveted among collectors.

2. The Golden Koala (Australia): The koala is an icon of Australian wildlife and appears on this gold coin. Each year, its design is updated, capturing the adorableness of this marsupial.

3. The Golden Panda (China): The Chinese Golden Panda is one of the most famous and recognizable coins in the world. With a design that changes annually, it depicts one of China's most beloved national treasures, the giant panda.

4. The Golden Dragon Coin (Australia): This 1 oz gold coin is a tribute to Chinese culture and the year of

the dragon. The design features an impressive Chinese dragon in artistic detail.

5. The Philippine Tamaraw (Philippines): This coin commemorates the rare tamaraw, an endangered species of water buffalo in the Philippines. Its beauty and rarity make it highly sought after by collectors.

6. The Gold Jaguar Coin (Mexico): This Mexican gold coin celebrates the jaguar, a legendary animal in Aztec culture. Its eye-catching design captures the strength and majesty of this creature.

7. The Malagasy Tiger (Madagascar): This coin from the island of Madagascar depicts a tiger. Its uniqueness and beauty make it one of the most sought-after coins in the Indian Ocean area.

8. The Lion of the British Empire (United Kingdom): This British coin celebrates the power of the British Empire with its iconic lion. Its design evokes a sense of grandeur and empire.

The Attraction of Exotic Coins: These exotic coins enchant collectors with their beauty, uniqueness, and the history they represent. They are not only valuable objects, but also windows into distant cultures and countries.

The Silver Kookaburra Coin

The Golden Panda   *The Lion of the British Empire*

The Philippine Tamarraw

The Golden Koala

Book 3

Scan the QR code below to access exclusive bonus content! Thank you for your support. I would appreciate it if you could leave a review on Amazon after exploring the book. Your feedback is crucial to me. Enjoy your continued reading and happy coin hunting!

Chapter 10: Bullion Coins – Investment in Precious Metals

Silver Bullion Coins: Investing in Silver

Silver bullion coins represent one of the most affordable and popular ways to invest in silver, a precious metal with a long history of intrinsic and industrial value. In this subchapter, we will explore the reasons why you should consider silver as part of your investment portfolio and delve into the different options available.

Why Invest in Silver

Silver has long been a haven for investors concerned about inflation and financial stability. Here are some reasons why you should consider investing in silver:

Diversification: Silver is an excellent way to diversify away from other financial assets, such as stocks and bonds. Its value is often not closely correlated with the stock market, which can provide a hedge against fluctuations in financial markets.

Protection from Inflation: Silver has been shown to preserve purchasing power over time. While governments can print additional currencies, silver has a limited supply, making it a haven against inflation.

Industrial Demand: Silver is widely used in industry, particularly in consumer technologies and renewable energy sectors. Growing demand from these sectors can positively influence the price of silver.

Portability and Liquidity: Silver bullion coins are easy to carry and sell. They are globally recognized and can be traded in many financial markets.

Numismatic History: Many collectors value silver bullion coins for their artistic beauty and the history they represent. Some silver bullion coins have additional numismatic value.

The Most Common Silver Bullion Coins

The most common silver bullion coins include:

American Silver Eagle: U.S. annual issuance of one troy ounce of pure silver.

Canadian Silver Maple Leaf: Canadian silver coins with high purity title.

Austrian Silver Philharmonic: Made in Austria, these coins are prized for their musical design.

Australian Silver Kangaroo: Minted in Australia, these silver coins show the famous kangaroo.

South African Krugerrand: Although originally designed in gold, there are now silver versions of these famous South African coins.

Tips for Buying Silver Bullion Coins

Before investing in silver bullion coins, keep these tips in mind:

Purity Rating: Make sure you know the purity of the silver in the coins you are buying. The standard purity is 999 silver, but there may be differences.

Authenticity Verification: To avoid counterfeits, buy from reliable sources and consider authenticity verification through certification services.

Purchase Costs: Consider the costs associated with the purchase, including the purchase price itself, commissions, and shipping costs.

Proper Storage: Once acquired, store silver coins properly to preserve their integrity and value.

Silver bullion coins offer an affordable way for investors and collectors to enter the world of precious metals. By choosing the right coins and following the right investment practices, silver can play an important role in your financial portfolio.

Gold Bullion Coins: The Gold Investment

Gold, with its eternal appeal, represents one of the world's most coveted precious metals. In this subchapter, we will explore why gold bullion coins are such a popular investment choice and what options are available to those who wish to invest in this precious metal.

Why Invest in Gold

Gold has been a stable store of value and a safe haven for centuries. Here are some reasons why you should consider investing in gold:

Value Stability: Gold is known to maintain its value over time, often functioning as insurance against stock market fluctuations and economic instabilities.

Diversification: Gold is an excellent form of portfolio diversification because its value is often uncorrelated with the stock and bond markets.

Protection from Inflation: Gold has proven to be an effective protection against inflation, as its value tends to rise when the purchasing power of currencies falls.

Universal Acceptance: Gold is recognized worldwide as a valuable commodity. Gold bullion coins are easily traded in financial markets around the globe.

History and Numismatics: Many gold bullion coins are also valued by collectors for their artistic design and history. Some of these coins have additional numismatic value.

Tips for Buying Gold Bullion Coins

When you decide to invest in gold bullion coins, consider these tips:

Purity: Make sure you know the purity of the gold in the coins you are buying. Bullion gold is often 99.9 percent pure.

Trust the Source: Buy from reliable sources and consider verifying authenticity through certification services.

Associated Costs: In addition to the purchase price, consider commissions and shipping costs.

Proper Storage: Once acquired, store gold coins properly to maintain their value.

Gold bullion coins offer a stable investment option and a valuable form of diversification for your portfolio. When you select the right coins and follow best investment practices, gold can play an essential role in your financial strategy.

Other Bullion Coins: Platinum, Palladium, and Alternative Precious Metals

In the world of coin collecting and investing, the focus is not only on gold and silver. This subchapter will explore the world of alternative precious metals, focusing particularly on platinum and palladium.

Platinum: The Precious "Cousin" of Gold

Platinum is a precious metal with unique characteristics. It is rarer than gold and is known for its high density and resistance to corrosion. Platinum is often used in jewelry and industrial applications, but platinum bullion coins are gaining popularity among investors. Here are some reasons to consider investing in platinum coins:

Scarcity: Platinum is much rarer than gold, which contributes to the high demand for this precious metal.

Industrial Applications: Platinum is widely used in industries such as automotive, electronics, and chemicals. Increasing industrial demand could positively influence its value.

Diversification: Investing in platinum coins can provide valuable portfolio diversification, as platinum often reacts differently than gold and silver to market changes.

Palladium: Platinum's Little Brother

Palladium is also a precious metal with properties similar to platinum. However, palladium is best known for its applications in the automotive industry, particularly in catalytic converters. This metal has recently attracted the attention of investors due to its growing demand and limited sources of mining.

Investing in palladium coins can offer several advantages:

Increasing Demand: As pollution regulations become more stringent and the production of low-emission vehicles increases, the demand for palladium is likely to grow.

Diversification: Investing in palladium can help diversify the portfolio because its performance is not closely correlated with that of gold or silver.

Other Alternative Precious Metals

In addition to platinum and palladium, there are other alternative precious metals, such as rhodium, ruthenium, and iridium, which are used in industrial and electronic applications. Although their availability in the form of bullion coins is limited, it is important to be aware of these options to fully understand the precious metals landscape.

Investing in alternative precious metals can offer unique opportunities, but it is essential to be informed and consider the risks associated with each metal. The choice between gold, silver, platinum, palladium, or other precious metals will depend on your financial goals, your comfort level, and your investment strategy.

Continue to explore the world of precious metals and bullion coins to create a diversified and balanced portfolio.

Gold and Silver Bullion: Investing in Solid Form

In the world of coin and precious metal investing and collecting, gold and silver bars are an alternative to bullion coins. These solid blocks of precious metal offer several advantages and are popular with investors for various reasons.

Benefits of Investing in Ingots

Guaranteed Purity: Gold and silver bars are often available with a purity of 99.9% or higher. This purity is guaranteed by the minting body and gives them a high value.

Different Cuts: Ingots come in different sizes and weights, allowing investors to choose the option that best suits their financial needs. You can find ingots from one gram up to one kilogram or more.

Ease of Storage: Ingots take up less space than coins, making them easy to store in a safe place such as a safe deposit box or storage room.

Liquidity: Gold and silver bars are easily traded around the world. Many companies that specialize in buying and selling precious metals accept bullion, ensuring a high degree of liquidity.

Differences between Ingots and Bullion Coins

It is important to note that there are some key differences between investing in bullion and investing in bullion coins:

Design and History: Bullion coins often feature eye-catching designs and may have additional collector value. Bullion, on the other hand, is generally less ornate and tends to be considered primarily for its intrinsic value.

Purchase Costs: Bullion coins may incur slightly higher purchase costs due to design and minting. Bullion coins are often less expensive at the time of purchase.

Taxation: Taxation on coins and bullion can vary depending on local laws and jurisdictions. It is important to understand the tax implications of investing in both forms.

Tips for Investing in Ingots

Research: Before buying gold or silver bars, perform thorough research on reputable buyers and minting organizations. Make sure the bars are authentic and meet stated purity standards.

Safe Storage: Because bullion can represent considerable value, it is essential to store it in a safe place. Many people choose safes or secure storage facilities for this purpose.

Liquidity: Although ingots are highly liquid, consider the ease of reselling them when choosing the size of ingots to purchase.

Investing in gold and silver bullion can be a solid option for diversifying your precious metals portfolio. Keep in mind the advantages and differences from bullion coins and plan your investment according to your financial goals.

Strategies for Investing in Bullion Coins

When it comes to investing in bullion coins, it is essential to develop a thoughtful strategy to maximize profits and reduce risk. Here are some key strategies that can help you better manage your bullion coin portfolio:

1. Diversification:

Diversifying your portfolio is essential. Buy a variety of gold and silver bullion coins of different sizes and series. In this way, you will reduce the risk associated with a single coin type or size and increase the overall liquidity of your portfolio.

2. Periodic Purchase:

One of the most common strategies is periodic purchasing. Establish a monthly or annual budget for purchasing bullion coins and maintain this plan over time. This allows you to take advantage of the benefits of time-weighted average cost.

3. Beware of Premiums and Spreads:

Premiums are the difference between the market price of the metal and the selling price of the coin. Spreads are the price differences between buying and selling. Look for coins with competitive premiums and spreads to maximize your return.

4. Monitor Markets:

Keep up with market conditions. Monitor gold and silver price trends and industry trends. This will help you make informed decisions about buying and selling your coins.

5. Purchase from Reliable Sources:

Buy bullion coins only from reputable sources. Turning to reputable dealers and companies that specialize in selling precious metals is a guarantee of authenticity and value.

6. Safe Storage:

Be sure to store your bullion coins in a safe place. A safe deposit box in a bank or a precious metals depository are ideal options. Proper storage preserves the value and integrity of your coins.

7. Strategic Selling:

Choose the right time to sell your bullion coins. Take into account market conditions and your financial goals. For example, you might decide to sell when prices reach a certain level or when you need liquidity.

8. Taxation:

Understand the tax implications of investing in bullion coins in your country of residence. Some jurisdictions may levy taxes on transactions or sales of precious metals.

The key to successful bullion coin investing is planning and strategy. Every investor will have a different approach based on his or her goals and market conditions. With a thoughtful strategy and a good understanding of the markets, you can benefit from investing in bullion coins as part of your overall financial portfolio.

The Future of Precious Metals Investment

Investing in precious metals, including bullion coins, is a practice with deep roots in history. But what is the future of this type of investment? Let's look at some of the important trends and considerations for the future of precious metals investing:

1. Growing Global Demand:

Global demand for precious metals, particularly gold and silver, continues to grow. Countries such as China and India are among the leading consumers of gold, and this demand is likely to remain strong. Growing economic prosperity and a growing middle class in these regions contribute to this demand.

2. Role as a "Refugee Value":

Precious metals often play the role of "safe haven value" in times of economic turmoil or global instability. Investors seek refuge in precious metals when financial markets are uncertain. This role as a "safe haven" is likely to continue.

3. Growth of Online Investment:

The growth of online investment platforms has made investing in precious metals more accessible. Investors can now buy and sell bullion coins from anywhere in the world with ease. This trend will continue to reduce barriers to entry for investors.

4. New Technologies:

New technologies, such as blockchain, are entering the precious metals sector. These technologies can be used to track the authenticity and provenance of coins, improving transparency and security for investors.

5. Digital Bullion Coins:

Innovation is leading to the creation of digital bullion coins. These are digital representations of physical coins and offer greater liquidity and flexibility. However, it is important to pay attention to potential threats related to security and regulation.

6. Fiscal Implications:

The tax implications of investing in precious metals may vary from country to country. Investors should be aware of local tax laws that may affect their investments.

7. Monitor Market Trends:

Anyone investing in precious metals needs to be aware of market trends. This includes price trends, global supply and demand, and economic news that may influence prices.

In general, investment in precious metals, including bullion coins, remains a valuable component of a well-diversified investment portfolio. The future of this sector looks bright, with opportunities for investors to diversify and protect their assets. However, as with any form of investment, it is essential to conduct thorough research and plan carefully for the best results.

Chapter 11: Collecting for Passion: – The Art of Collecting Coins

The Heart of Collectibles: Collecting for Passion

Coin collecting is an engaging experience that can greatly enrich anyone's life. In this subchapter, I want to take you deep into the world of numismatic passion and give you the tools to successfully begin your adventure.

The Inexplicable Charm of Coins: Imagine holding an ancient coin in your hands. Look closely at the details, engravings, and patina of time. Pay attention to the stories and historical moments it represents. That feeling of wonder and fascination is what makes coins so special. If you want to start collecting coins, start here: with that emotional connection and intrinsic fascination that coins evoke.

The Quest for Uniqueness: Every numismatic collector is looking for unique and special coins. You can start by looking for coins that are rare or ancient or that have unique characteristics. Numismatic treasure hunting is an integral part of collecting.

Connecting with History: Coins are windows to the past. You can begin your collection by choosing a historical era or period of interest and looking for coins associated with it. For example, you might start by collecting coins from ancient Rome or the United States during the Civil War. This will allow you to immerse yourself in history as you collect.

The Collectors' Community: Join online or local collector communities. Participating in discussion forums, social media groups, or numismatic clubs will allow you to share experiences, learn from experts, and get valuable advice. Sharing your passion with other people can be extremely rewarding.

The Satisfaction of Creating a Personal Collection: Start with small steps. Buy coins that interest you and fit your budget. Each coin you add to your collection will help create a unique story. Keep a record of your acquisitions, noting when and where you obtained each coin. This log will become part of your collecting history.

Collecting for Everyone: Coin collecting is open to anyone with an interest. There is no need to be an expert in numismatics. All you need is passion and curiosity. Start your collection today!

In this subchapter, I have provided you with an overview of how to begin your adventure as a coin collector. Start with a coin that fascinates you and create your own personal collection. Remember, the real heart of collecting is your passion.

Beauty in the Collector's Eye: Appreciating Monetary Art

One of the greatest joys of coin collecting is the opportunity to immerse oneself in monetary art. Each coin is a small work of art, a masterpiece created with care and skill. In this subchapter, we will explore how to develop a critical eye for coin art and how to appreciate its beauty.

The Art of Coins: Coins are not just pieces of metal with figures on them. They are works of art in miniature. Every aspect of a coin, from the image to the layout, is designed with attention to detail. Learning to recognize and appreciate these artistic features can greatly enrich your experience as a collector.

Monetary Iconography: Coins are often decorated with images of historical figures, deities, national symbols, or scenes from daily life. By carefully examining these images, you can discover many fascinating details about the culture and history of the place where the coin was minted. For example, a Roman coin might depict an emperor in specific clothing, giving you an idea of the period in which it was minted.

Monetary Technique: In addition to image, coins often have a variety of technical features. The arrangement of the numerals, the type of metal used, and the engravings on the reverse can all contribute to the overall beauty of a coin. For example, coins minted with advanced techniques may feature striking and intricate details.

The Patina of Time: Many coins develop a patina over the years. This patina is the result of contact with the surrounding environment and can give the coin a unique appearance. Some collectors prefer coins with a natural patina, considering it part of their history.

Personal Appreciation: Every collector has unique artistic tastes. What might appeal to one may not appeal to another. Be open to your personal preferences and look for coins that inspire you and that you find beautiful. Your collection should be a reflection of your personal taste.

The Documentation of Monetary Art: Keep a record of coins you find particularly beautiful or significant. Write down what struck you in particular and why. This will help you develop a deeper appreciation for monetary art over time.

In the world of coins, there is an infinite amount of beauty to be discovered. In this subchapter, you learned how to recognize and appreciate the art of coins. Remember that beauty is subjective, so follow your heart and choose the coins that fascinate you most.

Stories of Passionate Collectors: Inspirations and Successes

Hearing the stories of other passionate collectors can be an incredible inspiration and an opportunity to learn from those who have already traveled the path you are on. In this subchapter, we will explore some stories of collectors who have achieved great success and made coin collecting a significant part of their lives.

From Beginner to Expert: Many of the stories of collectors begin like yours, with a curiosity about coins and a desire to learn. These collectors started from scratch, but with passion, dedication, and commitment, they became experts in their field. Listening to their journey can give you confidence as you embark on your collecting adventure.

The Charm of Rare Coins: The stories of great discoveries are often the most compelling. Collectors who have accidentally found a rare coin in a dollar bill or in a seemingly common lot tell exciting stories of how luck smiled on them. These tales prove that luck can knock on anyone's door.

The Collection of a Lifetime: Some collectors have devoted decades to their passions. Their stories testify to the durability and endurance of coin collecting. Collecting coins can become a deep connection to history, culture, and beauty, and these stories clearly demonstrate this.

Sharing the Passion: Coin collecting is not always a solitary activity. Many collectors join clubs or associations to share their passion with others. These communities provide opportunities for exchange, discussion, and friendship among people with similar interests.

The Influence of Collectors: Collectors' stories can have a lasting impact. Some have donated their collections to museums or institutions to share them with the world. Others have written books or conducted research to contribute to numismatic knowledge. These collectors have left an indelible imprint on the numismatic community.

Stories from passionate collectors are an essential part of the world of coins. By listening to them, you can gain inspiration and wisdom for your own personal collecting journey. Be open to the experiences of others and you may find new ways to enrich your collection and your understanding of coins.

The Collection as a Reflection of Yourself: Creating a Personal Connection

One of the joys of coin collecting is the ability to create a collection that reflects your personality, interests, and history. In this subchapter, we will explore how you can make a personal connection with your coin collection, making it a unique expression of yourself.

1. Choose a Meaningful Theme: The first key to making a personal connection with your collection is to select a theme that is close to your heart. This could be based on personal interests, such as history, art, culture, or geography. For example, if you are passionate about ancient history, you might focus on Roman or Greek coins.

2. Research and Learn: Once you have chosen your theme, devote yourself to extensive research. Study and learn all you can about the coins related to your theme. Discovering the history and context behind

each coin will enable you to appreciate them more deeply.

3. Connect the Collection to Your Life: Look for ways to connect your collection to your daily life. You might decide to collect coins from countries you have visited while traveling or coins issued in your birthday year. These personal connections make the collection more meaningful.

4. Keep a Collection Journal: Keeping a collection journal is a great way to record the details of each coin in your collection. You can note where and when you acquired a coin, what meanings it has for you, and any other relevant information. This journal will become a valuable document over time.

5. Share Your Passion: Sharing your passion for coins with other collectors can further enrich your personal connection to the collection. Join local numismatic clubs or online forums, attend exhibitions, and meet other enthusiasts who share your passion.

Creating a personal connection to your collection makes coin collecting a rewarding and meaningful experience. Each coin you add to your collection tells a part of your story and passions, creating a unique bond between you and the wonderful world of coins.

The Art of the Portfolio: Exchanges and Interactions with Other Collectors

Coin collecting is not only a solitary activity; it can also be an opportunity to interact with other enthusiasts. In this subchapter, we will explore how sharing your passion for coins with other collectors can enrich your experience.

Attend Exhibitions and Conventions: Numismatic exhibitions and conventions are great events to meet other collectors and share your discoveries. During these occasions, you can show off your collection, learn from others, and even trade.

Join Numismatic Clubs: Many cities have local numismatic clubs where you can meet other collectors on a regular basis. These clubs offer opportunities to discuss coins, listen to expert speakers, and participate in exchanges or auctions among members.

Online Forums: The Internet offers a large community of coin collectors around the world. Participating in online numismatic forums allows you to share your experiences, ask for advice, and maybe even make virtual exchanges.

Fairs and Markets: Numismatic fairs and markets are great places to meet vendors and other collectors. Here, you can explore a wide range of coins, ask questions, and learn from experts in the field.

Coin Exchanges: Coin collecting offers the opportunity to trade coins with other collectors. These exchanges can be very rewarding and can help you complete your collection or add unique pieces.

Creating Lasting Friendships: Coin collecting is not only about objects, but also about the people you meet along the way. Many lasting friendships are born out of shared passion for coins.

Interacting with other collectors is a valuable part of the world of coin collecting. The connections you make can enrich your overall knowledge and experience, making your numismatic journey even more rewarding.

Chapter 12: Coins as Investment – Winning Strategies

Investing in Coins: An Option to Consider

In the world of coins, investing can offer unique opportunities for long-term profit. In this subchapter, we will explore the idea of investing in coins and why you might consider it as part of your financial strategy. I will be specific in outlining the benefits, precautions, and key considerations for successful coin investing.

Coins as Investments - We will begin with a basic overview of coin investments, explaining how coins can form a significant part of a well-diversified financial portfolio.

Reasons for Investing in Coins - We will explore reasons why coins can be an attractive investment option. These include the historical stability of the numismatic market, portfolio diversification, and the opportunity to enjoy your passions while investing.

Types of Investment Coins - We will discuss the various types of coins that are ideal for investment. These may include gold and silver coins, ancient and rare coins, and modern coins minted in limited editions.

Diversification and Risk Management - Diversification is critical to successful investing. We will explain how to select a balanced mix of currencies to reduce risk and maximize potential profit.

Monitoring the Market - In the world of coins, prices can vary widely. You will learn how to monitor the numismatic market, spot trends, and take advantage of opportunities when they arise.

Selling Successfully - At the end, we will discuss strategies for selling your coins successfully and maximizing your return on investment. This includes identifying the right time to sell and managing fees.

This subchapter will provide a detailed analysis of the key benefits and considerations for anyone considering investing in coins. It will be an essential starting point for those seeking to create a successful investment strategy in the world of coins.

Investment Coins: What Makes Coins Attractive?

To be successful in coin investing, it is essential to understand what makes them attractive and how to select the right opportunities. In this subchapter, we will explore the characteristics that make coins a unique and attractive investment choice, providing concrete examples and practical advice.

History and Prestige - Coins carry with them a rich history and inherent prestige. For example, ancient coins with a significant historical connection can attract the interest of collectors and investors. Take the example of an ancient Roman coin with a commemorative inscription of a famous emperor: its value is often linked to its unique history.

Scarcity and Demand Factors - Scarcity is a key element in determining the value of coins. Coins with limited print runs or those that have become rare over time may increase in value. For example, gold coins issued in limited editions by a mint may become highly sought after by collectors and investors.

Inherent and Intrinsic Value - Some coins have an intrinsic value derived from their precious metal content, such as gold or silver. For example, a gold coin may have intrinsic value based on the amount of gold it contains, in addition to its numismatic value. This dual source of value can make some coins particularly attractive to investors.

Numismatic Market Historical Stability - The numismatic market has demonstrated historical stability over time. Even during periods of economic turbulence, quality numismatic coins often maintain their value or even appreciate. For example, during the 2008 recession, many gold and silver coins saw an increase in demand and value, serving as a safe haven for investors.

Portfolio Diversification - Coins can help diversify your overall portfolio. Including diverse assets, such as coins, can help reduce the overall risk of your portfolio. For example, if the stock market is declining, the value of numismatic coins may hold steady or even increase, helping to balance your portfolio.

Appreciation over Time - Well-selected coins can appreciate significantly over time. For example, a silver coin issued in the past may be worth much more than its face value today because of increasing demand from collectors and investors. These examples demonstrate how a judicious choice of coins over the years can lead to significant appreciation of your investment.

When considering coins as an investment option, keep these characteristics in mind and look for opportunities that incorporate them. Our goal is to give you the tools to make informed choices and build a numismatic coin portfolio that is attractive from an investment perspective. Throughout this book, we will explore these issues further and guide you in selecting the coins that best suit your financial goals.

Building a Coin Portfolio: Diversification and Risk Management

Diversification is one of the keys to success in coin investing. In this subchapter, we will explore the importance of diversification and risk management in building your coin portfolio.

Geographic Diversification - One of the first considerations in diversifying your numismatic portfolio is geographic diversification. Look for coins from different geographic regions or countries. For example, you can include coins from Europe, Asia, America, and Africa. This geographic diversification can help mitigate the risk associated with specific economic or political events in a region.

Diversification by Coin Type - In addition to geographic diversification, it is important to diversify by coin type. You can include gold, silver, copper, and other alloy coins. Also, consider coins from different eras, such as ancient, medieval, and modern. This diversification by coin type can help balance your portfolio.

Diversification by Category - Numismatic coins can be divided into several categories based on their characteristics and value. These categories can include commemorative coins, antique coins, precious metal investment coins, etc. Be sure to have a diverse representation among these categories.

Risk Management - In addition to diversification, it is important to consider risk management in your coin portfolio. Set clear goals and a budget for your coin investment. Also, consider capital allocation— i.e., how much you want to invest in coins relative to other assets in your portfolio.

Monitoring and Updates - Coin portfolio management also requires constant monitoring and the ability to make updates when necessary. Pay attention to market trends and emerging opportunities. If some coins are showing significant appreciation, you may decide to balance your portfolio further.

Diversification of Numismatic Risk - Not all coins are equal in terms of numismatic risk. Some coins may be more susceptible to market fluctuations than others. Do extensive research on the coins you are considering and look for those with a stable history of appreciation over time.

Diversification and risk management are key to preserving and growing the value of your coin portfolio. Also, keep in mind that diversification does not completely eliminate risk, but it can help you reduce it.

Numismatic Market: How to Monitor Trends and Opportunities

The ability to monitor market trends and recognize investment opportunities is crucial to success in numismatic coin investing. In this subchapter, we will explore strategies and tools that will enable you to maintain a clear view of the market and make informed decisions.

Stay Informed - One of the most important steps in monitoring the numismatic market is to stay constantly informed. Subscribe to trade journals, participate in online forums, and follow coin-related news. Maintaining a solid knowledge base is essential to identifying opportunities.

Catalogs and Valuation Guides - Use reliable catalogs and valuation guides to keep track of coin prices. These tools provide detailed information on the market values of coins based on various conditions and characteristics. It is important to use up-to-date and authoritative sources.

Numismatic Auctions - Numismatic auctions are great places to monitor market trends. Attending auctions or simply observing them allows you to assess the value of coins and see how the market responds to specific specimens. Auctions can also provide opportunities to purchase coins of interest.

Collectors' Groups - Joining local or online collectors' groups can be valuable. These groups often share information and experiences about the numismatic market. In addition, they can provide opportunities to make contacts with other collectors and investors.

Global Economic Indicators - Keep an eye on global economic indicators. Macroeconomic events such as inflation, interest rates, and currency fluctuations can affect the currency market. Learn how to interpret how these variables can affect the value of your currencies.

Search for New Opportunities - Don't limit yourself to coins with which you are familiar. Look for new investment opportunities by exploring coins from different eras or regions. Also, you might consider investing in commemorative coins or silver and gold coins, depending on market conditions.

Buying and Selling Strategy - Develop a buying and selling strategy based on your market knowledge and investment goals. Decide when is the right time to buy or sell your coins and maintain a disciplined approach.

Constant Evaluation - Finally, remember that the numismatic market is constantly evolving. This means you will need to constantly evaluate your portfolio and make updates based on new information and opportunities you encounter.

The ability to monitor the market and recognize investment opportunities is a critical skill for numismatic investors. By maintaining an informed and flexible view, you will be able to make sound decisions and increase your chances of success in coin investing.

Selling Successfully: Maximizing Return on Investment

Having a sound sales strategy is just as important as buying strategy in the world of coin collecting. In this subchapter, we will examine how to maximize your return on investment when it is time to sell your numismatic coins.

Assessing the Right Moment - The first key to successful selling is to assess the right moment. Carefully monitor the market and look for signs that indicate that the value of your coins has increased. These signs may include rising prices of similar coins or increasing demand for certain specimens.

Select Sales Channel - There are several options for selling your coins. You can approach auction houses, specialty dealers, online sellers, or participate in numismatic fairs. Your choice of channel will depend on your needs and the type of coins you are trying to sell.

Keep Documentation - Make sure you have complete and accurate documentation for your coins. This documentation can include certificates of authenticity, detailed descriptions, and high-quality photographs. Comprehensive documentation will help build buyer confidence and result in a better price.

Set a Fair Price - When setting the price of your coins, try to be fair and realistic. Consider the condition of the coin, rarity, market demand, and the commissions you may have to pay if you sell through brokers. A fair price will attract serious buyers.

Negotiation - In some cases, you may have to negotiate the price with potential buyers. Be prepared to approach the negotiation firmly but cooperatively. The goal is to reach an agreement that satisfies both parties.

Commissions and Costs - Remember that commissions or sales charges may apply, depending on the channel you choose. Consider these charges when calculating your return on investment.

Sales Tracking - Maintain a record of sales made, including details such as date of sale, price obtained, and associated expenses. This data will help you evaluate your performance and make future decisions.

Reinvesting Profits - After successfully selling your coins, consider whether you want to reinvest the profits in other numismatic coins or other investment opportunities. A well-considered strategy can help grow your portfolio further.

Consultation with an Expert - If you have any doubts or if you are dealing with high-value coins, it may be helpful to consult a numismatic expert or specialized attorney to ensure a legal and protected transaction.

Successfully selling your numismatic coins requires planning, preparation, and a good understanding of the market. With a well-defined strategy and attention to detail, you can maximize your return on investment and get maximum value from your coins.

Chapter 13: Winning Gestures for Your Coin Collection – Maximizing Value with the Appropriate Budget

Financial Planning for Collectors

Financial planning is the foundation upon which sound budgeting in your coin collection is built. Here we will explore the key steps to ensure that your approach to numismatics is financially sustainable.

Define Your Financial Goals

Before you start your collection, clearly define your financial goals. Do you want to collect for pleasure or for investment? Do you want to create a legacy to leave behind? These goals will help guide your financial decisions.

Assess Your Current Financial Situation

A realistic assessment of your financial situation is essential. Consider your income, your savings, and your debts. Determine how much you are willing to invest in your coin collection without putting your financial stability at risk.

Establish an Adequate Budget

Based on the financial assessment, establish a budget appropriate for your numismatic expenses. Make sure the budget includes not only the purchase of coins but also incidental expenses such as cases, insurance, and cataloging fees.

Consider Diversification

As in any financial strategy, diversification is key. Don't just focus on a single category of currencies. Explore different eras, types of coins, and currencies to reduce financial risk.

Plan for Long-Term Expenditures

Consider long-term expenses such as the cost of storage, coin maintenance, and taxes. These costs can increase over time, so plan for the future.

Consultation with a Financial Expert

If you have a coin collection of significant value, you may want to consult a financial expert or wealth advisor. They can help you develop a financial strategy that fits your needs.

Financial planning is the first step toward successful budgeting in coin collecting. This step will help you establish the solid financial foundation you need to enjoy your numismatic passion without putting your financial situation at risk.

Establish a Realistic Budget

Creating a budget is a crucial step in the financial management of a coin collection. Here's how to establish a realistic budget that will allow you to manage your expenses in a balanced way.

Analyze Your Current Finances

Before setting a budget, carefully analyze your current financial situation. Examine your monthly income, savings, debts, and fixed expenses. This overview will give you a clear idea of the financial resources available to you.

Define Specific Goals

Ask yourself what you want to get out of your coin collection. Do you want to collect for personal pleasure, or do you have investment goals? Setting specific goals will help you prioritize your spending.

Assign a Monthly or Annual Budget

Based on your financial situation and goals, assign a monthly or annual budget for your numismatic expenses. Make sure this budget is realistic and sustainable over the long term.

Consider Ancillary Expenses

In your budget, don't forget to include incidental expenses, such as protective coin cases, insurance, and cataloging costs. These often-overlooked details can accumulate over time.

Reserve a Fund for Unexpected Opportunities

In addition to your regular budget, it is wise to set aside a fund for unexpected opportunities or valuable coins that might appear in the market. This will give you the flexibility to seize unique opportunities.

Maintain a Constant Review

The budget is not fixed and unchanging. Keep a constant review and make changes if necessary. Adapt to financial circumstances and developments in your collection.

Be Disciplined

Once you have set a budget, be disciplined in sticking to it. Avoid going over the set budget, as this could put your financial situation at risk.

Establishing a realistic budget is essential to maintaining financial control in your coin collection. This will help you enjoy your passion in a responsible and sustainable way.

Smart Investments in Coins: Building a Successful Collection

Investing in coins can be a fascinating and profitable financial strategy. However, to get the most out of your investments, it is essential to follow an informed and thoughtful approach. In this subchapter, we will explore the key steps to building a successful coin collection that works as both a source of personal pleasure and a smart investment.

Combining Passion and Investment

First, recognize that coin collecting can be both a personal passion and an investment. The passion part can guide you to coins that fascinate you, while the investment part will require you to consider the coins' potential value over time. Finding a balance between these two aspects is essential to a successful collection.

Continuing Education

One of the most important steps is education. Study the coin market, learn from authoritative sources, and stay abreast of industry trends and developments. Knowledge is your best ally in making informed investment decisions.

Establish a Realistic Budget

Set a realistic budget for your numismatic acquisitions. It is easy to get caught up in the auction frenzy or exceptional coins, but having a budget will help you avoid impulsive purchases that could put your financial situation at risk.

Portfolio Diversification

As with any other type of investment, diversification is crucial. Do not concentrate all your funds on a single coin or type of currency. Expand your portfolio with different coins and numismatic categories to reduce risk.

Monitor the Market

Keep an eye on the coin market and trends. Some coins may appreciate faster than others. Gather information on coins that show potential for future growth.

Focus on High-Quality Coins

The quality of the coin is crucial. Well-preserved and authentic coins are often more attractive to collectors and investors. Investing in high-quality coins could result in steady growth in value.

Buy and Research Historical Coins

Coins with strong historical significance or those sought after by collectors tend to maintain or increase in value. Look for coins related to historical events or people of numismatic interest.

Long-Term Planning

Coin investments require a long-term perspective. Do not expect quick gains. Plan to invest over time and hold coins for extended periods to maximize their appreciation potential.

Consulting Experts

If you feel unsure about your investment decisions, consider consulting numismatic experts or professionals in the field. They can offer valuable advice based on experience and market knowledge.

Risk Management

As with any investment, understand the associated risks and be prepared to manage them. Never invest more than you are willing to lose. Consider diversifying your portfolio further to reduce risk.

Creating a successful coin collection that works both as a source of personal pleasure and as a smart investment requires a well-thought-out approach. With the right planning and a good dose of passion, you can maximize the potential of your coins as an investment.

The Coin Market: When to Buy and Sell Successfully

Navigating the coin market requires a thorough understanding of the dynamics of buying and selling. In this subchapter, we will explore the best time to acquire coins for your collection and when you might consider selling to maximize your investment.

Your Buying Strategy

Before making a purchase, it is essential to have a clear strategy in mind. Plan whether you are looking for specific coins, want to expand a particular part of your collection, or simply want to explore new opportunities.

The Importance of Research

You cannot stress enough how important research is. Monitor auctions, fairs, and specialty stores to get an idea of market prices and trends. Keep track of price changes for coins that interest you.

Buying in Low Market Periods

Buying coins during low market periods can be a good strategy. During such periods, you may be able to find bargains and discounts on coins that would normally be more expensive. Monitor market fluctuations and act when prices fall.

Cunning in the Auctions

Auctions can offer exceptional coins, but they require cunning. Learn the rules of auctions and how to participate effectively. Set a price limit before the auction and stick to it to avoid going over your budget.

Selling in Times of High Demand

If you wish to sell part of your collection, look for times when demand for certain coins is high. For example, some coins may be in particular demand at a time in history or to commemorate an event.

Giving Up Coins with Profit

If you have coins that have seen significant appreciation, you might consider selling them to cash in on the profit. However, always try to balance the desire for profit with the love of your collection. Some coins may have personal significance beyond their financial value.

Avoid Impulsive Sales

Never sell impulsively. Even in difficult times, take the time to consider whether selling is really in the long-term interest of your collection and your financial goals.

The Importance of a Professional Evaluation

When you have rare or high-value coins, consider getting a professional appraisal. Numismatic experts can help you determine the current value of your coins and make informed decisions about selling them.

Selling with a Plan in Mind

If you have decided to sell part of your collection, make a plan. Choose whether you want to sell through a dealer, an auction, or directly to other collectors. Plan your selling strategy in advance.

Knowledge and Flexibility

Market knowledge is critical, but flexibility is equally important. The coin market is constantly changing, and what works today may not work tomorrow. Be willing to adapt to new circumstances and opportunities.

Understanding the right time to buy or sell coins is an essential part of success in the numismatic world. Make the most of market opportunities and be strategic in your buying and selling decisions.

How to Avoid Unnecessary Expenses in Your Coin Collection

Careful budget management is critical to the success and longevity of your coin collection. In this subchapter, we will explore strategies to avoid unnecessary spending and maximize the value of every dollar you invest in your numismatic passion.

Define Your Budget

The first step in avoiding unnecessary spending is to establish a clearly defined budget. Consider how much you are willing to invest in your coin collection and stick to this limit. A well-planned budget helps you avoid impulse purchases and maintain control over your finances.

Do Research Prior to Purchase

Before making any purchase, devote yourself to research. Find out the value of the coins you are interested in and explore the market, auctions, and dealers. Knowledge puts you in a better position to make informed decisions and avoid overpriced purchases.

Beware of Commissions and Additional Costs

When participating in auctions or buying from dealers, consider commissions and additional costs. These costs can increase the price of a coin significantly. Pay attention to how much you will have to pay in total for a given purchase.

Avoid Too Much Too Soon

Do not be hasty in purchasing a coin. Before committing your money, consider whether the coin is really what you are looking for and whether the price is fair. Special offers and promotions can be tempting, but don't get caught up in the rush.

Buy Only Authentic Coins

Counterfeiting is a problem in the coin world, and buying counterfeit coins can be an unnecessary expense. Before making a purchase, make sure the coin is genuine. Working with reputable dealers and obtaining numismatic certifications can help you avoid problems.

Plan Ahead

Plan your purchases in advance. If you have a list of coins you want to add to your collection, you can patiently search for them and wait for the best opportunities. This will help you avoid impulsive and expensive purchases.

Avoid Excessive Accumulation

It is easy to get caught up in numismatic passion and accumulate too many coins. Keep in mind that every coin requires space, care, and maintenance. Avoid hoarding and focus your efforts on coins that you really want and that fit into your collection plan.

Evaluate Your Existing Coin Portfolio

Periodically, take time to evaluate the coins you already own. This will allow you to identify coins you may want to sell to make room for new purchases or to reinvest in more valuable coins.

Buy in Reasonable Quantities

Buying coins in excessive quantities can be expensive. Be careful not to overdo it, especially if your budget is limited. Better to own a few high-quality coins than many low-value coins.

Be Selective and Excellent in Your Choice

Finally, be selective in your purchasing choices. Look for exceptional and valuable coins that will truly enrich your collection. Do not fall into the trap of buying common or uninteresting coins just because they are cheap.

Careful budget management is a key element to a rewarding numismatic experience. With a well-planned budget and attention to detail, you can avoid unnecessary expenses and build a coin collection of lasting value.

The Balance of Passion and Financial Prudence in Your Coin Collection

Maintaining a balance between your passion for numismatics and financial prudence is essential for successful budget management of your coin collection. In this subchapter, we will explore how to cultivate a financially responsible mindset as you continue to pursue your passion for coins.

Set Clear Goals

Before you begin any purchase, set clear goals for your coin collection. What do you wish to achieve with this collection? Do you want to collect coins from a specific historical period? Or perhaps you are interested in a particular geographic region? Setting clear goals will help you focus your efforts and avoid impulse purchases.

Plan Your Budget

Budget planning is critical. Evaluate how much you are willing to invest annually in your collection and respect this limit. A budget protects you from overspending and ensures that you can continue to cultivate your passion in a sustainable way.

Avoid Impulsive Purchasing

Auctions and coin markets can be irresistible, but avoid impulse purchases. Take the time to research, compare prices, and carefully evaluate each purchase. In this way, you will avoid coin purchases you may later regret.

Keep a Detailed Record

Keep a detailed record of your numismatic expenditures. Record each purchase, including price, date, and a description of the coin. This allows you to keep track of your investments and evaluate the progress of your collection over time.

Make Trading and Sales Smart

Periodically, evaluate your collection and consider selling or trading coins that may no longer match your goals. Well-planned sales or trades can help you free up funds to acquire more desirable coins.

Involve a Professional

If your collection reaches a certain value, you may want to bring in a professional to appraise your coins and provide financial advice. A numismatic expert can help you make informed decisions.

Avoid Financial Over-Commitment

Although it is exciting to look for new and rare coins, avoid over-committing yourself financially. Make sure you can afford the coins you buy so as not to jeopardizeyour financial stability.

Stay Informed About the Market

The coin market is constantly changing. Stay informed about trends and price fluctuations. This knowledge helps you make financially intelligent decisions.

Passion Must Prevail

Finally, remember that passion is at the heart of coin collecting. Keep your passion alive while following financially responsible stewardship. The balance between passion and financial prudence allows you to fully enjoy your numismatic experience.

Maintaining a balance between your passion for coins and prudent financial management is the key to a successful and lasting collection. With careful planning, you can cultivate your passion without compromising your financial stability.

Chapter 14: Your Long-Term Collection – Preservation and Succession

Preserving Your Heritage: Long-Term Conservation

One of the most critical aspects of coin collecting is the long-term preservation of your collection. In this subchapter, we will examine best practices for preserving your numismatic heritage for future generations.

Proper Storage Environment - The first step in long-term storage is to make sure that coins are stored in a suitable environment. Fluctuations in temperature, humidity, and exposure to sunlight can damage coins. Use cases and containers designed specifically for numismatic storage and store coins in a cool, dry, and dark place.

Handle Coins Carefully - When you have to handle coins, be sure to do so with care. Use cotton gloves to avoid leaving fingerprints and handle coins only by the edges. Coins should be lifted gently and never touched directly on the surface.

Avoid Excessive Cleaning - Resist the temptation to over-clean coins. Improper cleaning can damage the patina and surface of coins, reducing their value. If necessary, consult a numismatic professional about cleaning.

Organization and Cataloging - Keep accurate records of your collection, including details such as date of acquisition, provenance, and specific characteristics of the coins. A well-organized cataloging system will help you keep track of your coins and facilitate succession.

Security and Insurance - Make sure your collection is protected from theft, fire, or natural disaster. Invest in a quality safe to store coins securely and consider purchasing insurance specifically for the collection to protect its financial value.

Succession Planning - If you want your collection to continue to be a significant part of the family estate, plan for succession. Involve your family in your intentions and make sure they are aware of the coins and their importance.

Periodic Appraisal - Conduct periodic appraisals of your collection. The value of coins may change over time, and you may wish to make changes to your storage or sales strategy based on these appraisals.

Long-term preservation of numismatic coins requires dedication and attention to detail. With judicious handling and proper precautions, you can ensure that your collection remains in pristine condition and continues to bring satisfaction to you and future generations.

Passing the Witness: Planning the Succession of the Collection

An often overlooked aspect of coin collecting is succession planning for your collection. While many collectors are passionate about their coins during their lifetime, it is important to consider what will happen to the collection once it is passed on to future generations or sold. In this subchapter, we will examine key considerations for planning the succession of your numismatic collection.

Involve Your Family - The first and most important consideration is to involve your family in your intentions. Make sure they are aware of your collection, its value, and your vision for its future. Talk openly with family members to see if anyone is interested in continuing the collection.

Document the Collection - Maintain detailed documentation of your collection, including inventories, photos, and information on the provenance of coins. This documentation will be invaluable to those who inherit the collection or to a future buyer.

Define a Succession Plan - Decide who should inherit the collection and in what manner. If you have multiple heirs, consider whether you want the collection divided among them or kept as a single entity. A well-defined succession plan can avoid disputes and uncertainty in the future.

Ongoing Conservation and Security - Ensure that those who inherit the collection are aware of the conservation and security practices necessary to keep the collection in good condition. Provide contact information of trusted numismatic professionals in case advice is needed.

Periodic Valuation - Even if you have planned for succession, it is important to conduct periodic valuations of your collection. Coin values may change over time, and you may wish to make changes to your succession plan based on these evaluations.

Selling Options - If no family member is interested in inheriting the collection, consider selling options.

You may decide to sell the collection at a numismatic auction or through a specialized broker. Alternatively, you can establish instructions to sell the collection after your passing and use the proceeds for specific purposes.

Consider Charities or Museums - If you want your collection to have a lasting impact, you might consider donating some or all of your coins to charities or numismatic museums. This is a noble option that can preserve your numismatic legacy for the future.

Planning the succession of your numismatic collection requires care and thought. Be sure to involve your family in the process and keep your plan updated as your circumstances or intentions change.

Creating a Family Bond: Involving the Family in the Collection

Coin collecting can be a lonely passion, but involving your family in your collection can enrich the experience and ensure the preservation of your numismatic legacy for future generations. In this subchapter, we will explore how to involve your family members in your passion for coins.

Involve Children - If you have children or grandchildren, involving them in your collection can spark interest and appreciation for coins from a young age. Show them the coins, tell interesting stories about their origin and history, and maybe give them special coins to start their collection.

Involve Spouse or Partner - Talk to your spouse or partner about your intentions for your collection and explain to them both the sentimental and potentially financial value of the coins. Involving them in the management and preservation of the collection can contribute to better understanding and collaboration.

Organize Coin-Related Family Events - Organize coin-related family events such as cataloging nights, visits to numismatic exhibitions, or even excursions to coin-related historical sites. These events can strengthen family bonding through common interest.

Show the Educational Aspect - Emphasize the educational aspect of coin collecting. Coins are a window into history, geography, and culture, and involving the family can be a fun way to learn together.

Involve Family Members in Succession Decisions - If you plan to pass your collection on to specific family members, involve them in the decisions and plans. Ask them which coins they would prefer to inherit and explain your reasons.

Encourage Active Participation - If someone in your family shows a genuine interest in coin collecting, encourage them to actively participate in the collection. They can help with cataloging, research, or participation in numismatic exhibitions.

Document Family History with Coins - Use coins as a means of documenting family history. For example, you could create a special set of coins commemorating important family events, such as weddings or births.

Involving your family in your numismatic collection can create stronger bonds among family members and preserve your numismatic heritage for future generations.

The Evolution of Your Collection: Updates and Enhancements

A numismatic collection is constantly evolving, and this subchapter will explore how you can update and improve your collection over time. The goal is to make your collection richer, more meaningful, and more fascinating as you gain experience in coin collecting.

Upgrades and New Purchases - Keep your collection interesting by adding new coins. Purchase pieces that fit your evolving interests or complement the themes of your existing collection.

Expand Knowledge - Deepen your knowledge of coins. Learn more about the characteristics, history, and variations of the coins you collect. This knowledge will help you make more informed decisions about future purchases.

Restoration and Enhancement - In some cases, you may want to restore or enhance the coins in your collection. This may involve professional cleaning or correcting minor defects. Be sure to do this only with coins that will not lose value as a result of the work.

Participation in Exhibitions - Showcase your collection by participating in local or national numismatic exhibitions. These exhibitions will give you the opportunity to share your passion with other collectors and receive valuable feedback.

Networking with Other Collectors - Continue to build your network of contacts with other collectors. Networking can lead to interesting exchanges, buying opportunities, and new friendships with similar interests.

Numismatic Club Participation - Join local or online numismatic clubs. These clubs often offer events, resources, and connections that can enhance your collecting experience.

Updates in Conservation - Keep your conservation skills current. Best conservation practices can change over time, so it is important to stay informed of the latest developments.

Succession Planning - Continue to plan for the succession of your collection. As the collection grows in value, it is important to make sure your succession intentions are clear and well documented.

Creating Special Sets - Consider creating special sets within your collection. These may include particularly rare coin sets or unique numismatic themes.

The evolution of your numismatic collection is an integral part of the collecting experience. This subchapter has provided you with suggestions on how you can continue to improve your collection over time.

The Legacy of a Collection: Stories and Values

Every numismatic collection has a story to tell, and in this subchapter, we will explore the deeper meaning of your coins and how they might influence the future. Consider this as a time to reflect on what your collection represents to you and how it might influence future generations.

Passing on Knowledge and Passion - Your collection is not only a collection of coins, but also a source of knowledge and passion. Think about how you can pass this knowledge and passion on to your family members or heirs. You can do this through discussions, written guides, or even the inclusion of your heirs in numismatic activities.

Documenting History - Be sure to document the history of your coins. This can include recording the individual histories of each coin, where they came from, and your collecting experiences. These details can enrich the history of your collection.

Values and Meanings - Reflect on the deeper meaning of the coins in your collection. What do they represent to you? What values, ideals, or memories are associated with them? These meanings may be important for future generations.

Inheritance Planning - If you plan to leave your collection as an inheritance, it is critical to plan ahead. Consult a legal expert or financial advisor to ensure that your collection is managed and distributed according to your wishes.

Family Stories - Coins can become an integral part of your family history. Think about how family stories can be interwoven with your collection and how they can be passed down through the generations.

Valuing Preservation - Continue to invest in preserving your coins so that they can remain in optimal condition for future generations. This may include using professional services or educating your heirs about coin stewardship.

Share the Stories - Talk about the stories of your coins with your loved ones and share your passion with them. This can help preserve the meaning of coins even after your generation.

Monetaries of the Future - Consider how future collectors in your family might develop an interest in coins. You could be the springboard for a new generation of numismatists.

This subchapter explores the more personal and enduring side of your numismatic collection. By reflecting on the values, history, and stories associated with your coins, you can ensure that your collection leaves a meaningful legacy for future generations.

Book 4

Chapter 15: Essential Guide to Managing Inherited Coins

Heirs of Coins: Valuation and Preservation

Inheriting a coin collection is a significant event that requires attention and care. This subchapter offers detailed guidance on how to value and preserve inherited coins while preserving their historical, artistic, and economic value.

Initial Assessment: Discovering Family Treasure

The first step in managing inherited coins is an initial assessment. You may be faced with a box of coins or a well-organized collection, but in either case, it is important to know what you have. This can involve:

Examine Coins: Carefully examine each coin, noting their condition, date, place of issue, and potential market value.

Catalog: Create a detailed catalog of inherited coins, including any associated historical or family information.

Preliminary Research: Conduct basic research on coins to get a general idea of their value and historical significance.

Value Assessment: Professionals or Experts

After the initial appraisal, it is essential to determine the value of the coins. This may require the help of a numismatic expert or professional numismatist, especially if the collection is complex or contains rare coins. The expert will examine:

Condition: The condition of the coin is critical to its value. The expert will evaluate scratches, wear, cleaning marks, stains, and other imperfections.

Rarity: Determine whether coins are common or rare. Coins that are rare or minted in limited numbers may be worth considerably more.

History: Coins with an interesting history or provenance may have additional value.

Current Market: The value of coins may vary over time depending on the current numismatic market.

Preservation: Care for the Future

Once coins have been appraised, it is critical to take care of them to preserve their value and integrity over time. Here are some key steps:

Adequate Cleaning: If necessary, clean the coins carefully, avoiding damage to them.

Storage: Use high-quality numismatic cases or albums to protect coins from dust and moisture.

Handle with Care: When you must handle coins, use numismatic gloves to avoid direct contact with your fingers.

Insurance: Insures coins in case of theft or physical damage.

Contemporary Research: Continue to monitor the market value of coins and consult experts as needed.

This subchapter provides the information needed to value and preserve legacy coins responsibly and consciously, maximizing their value in both financial and historical terms.

Keeping the Family Connection with Historic Coins Alive - Stories, Memories, and the Beauty of the Numismatic Legacy

In the second subchapter, we will explore how inherited historical coins can be used to keep family ties alive by passing on stories, memories, and the beauty of numismatic heritage.

Stories in Coins: Transmitting Family Memories

Coins often encapsulate stories that can be passed from generation to generation. The second subchapter will examine how historical coins tell a part of family history. These stories may be about coin acquisition, travel, collecting, or even important historical events. Sharing these stories with family members can create a meaningful link between generations.

Engraved Memories: Coins as Memory Bearers

Coins often serve as tangible reminders of significant events in an individual's life or of a past era. In the second subchapter, we will explore how coins can act as memory bearers, reminding all family members of important events, traditions, or the passions of the original collector.

The Beauty of the Numismatic Legacy

The intrinsic beauty of historical coins is another aspect that will be covered. The subchapter will explain how coins can be appreciated not only for their financial value, but also for their aesthetic beauty. It will show how the aesthetics of coins can become a focal point for sharing and appreciation within the family.

How to Involve the Family

A key aspect of this subchapter will be how to involve all family members in the appreciation and preservation of historic coins. This may include activities such as family coin viewing sessions, creating numismatic albums, or participating in coin-related exhibitions and events. Practical suggestions will be offered on how to involve people of different ages.

A Lasting Bond

The second subchapter will address the importance of creating a lasting bond with inherited historical coins. This will not only help preserve the family heritage, but also create unique opportunities for the family to connect through a shared passion for numismatics. It will emphasize how the beauty of the coins and the stories they tell can help create a lasting bond among family members, generation after generation.

Winning Strategies for Selling Inherited Coins - Maximize Return with Smart Options

When you find yourself managing an inherited coin collection, maximizing the financial return requires a series of thoughtful decisions and judicious actions. Here is a detailed guide on how to proceed effectively:

Professional Appraisal: Accurate appraisal of inherited coins is critical. The first step is to consult a numismatic expert. This professional can determine the value of each coin based on factors such as rarity, condition, and market demand. Be sure to obtain a written estimate from a trusted professional.

Proper Storage: Keeping coins in optimal condition is essential. Purchase protective cases for each coin to prevent physical damage. Avoid cleaning coins improperly, as this may damage them irreparably.

Documentation: Accompany each coin with thorough documentation. This can include certificates of authenticity, historical provenance, or any other relevant information. Solid documentation can increase buyer confidence.

Market Choice: Consider the different market options available. These include physical auctions, online auctions, private sales, and numismatic stores. Each option has advantages and disadvantages, so choose the one that best suits your needs.

Auction Sale: If you decide to participate in an auction, select a reputable auction house. Work with them to establish an appropriate reserve price and determine if you want an unreserved or minimum reserve sale.

Private Sale: Selling directly to a private buyer is another option. Post detailed ads online or target potential buyers through numismatic forums or social groups. Be sure to negotiate the price effectively and document the deal.

Online Platforms: If you choose online platforms such as eBay or others specific to numismatists, create accurate and detailed listings for each coin. Use high-quality images and provide all necessary information.

Tax Optimization: Consult a tax professional to understand the tax implications of selling. In some cases, you may be subject to capital gains taxes.

Smart Negotiation: Be patient and prepared to negotiate price with potential buyers. Knowing the value of your coins will give you an edge in negotiations.

Family Planning: Involve your family in this process. If you are managing an inherited collection, it is important to consider the expectations and wishes of all family members. Involve them in the decision to sell or keep the coins.

Protection of Memories: Even if selling is the main goal, remember that these coins may have sentimental value to your family. Preserve the stories and memories associated with the coins.

Communication with Professionals: Work with experts, such as probate lawyers or financial advisers, to address any legal or financial issues related to inheritance.

By carefully following these strategies and making informed decisions, you can maximize the financial return from the sale of legacy coins while preserving the historical and sentimental value of this collection.

Donating Inherited Coins in a Meaningful Way - Charitable and Beneficial Options

If you have decided that donating inherited coins is the right choice for you and your family, there are several charitable and beneficial options that can give deeper meaning to this action. Here's how you can proceed in a meaningful way:

Identifying Organizations: The first thing to do is to identify charities or charitable organizations that reflect the values and interests of the deceased or your family. This could include local, national, or international charitable organizations with a significant impact in the coins' sphere of interest.

Contact Organizations: Once you have identified organizations, contact them directly. Explain your intention to donate legacy coins and ask about the procedures for accepting donations. Some organizations may have specific procedures for accepting valuable assets such as coins.

Professional Appraisal: Before proceeding with the donation, have the coins appraised by an experienced numismatist. This appraisal will enable you to know the financial value of the coins, which is important for tax registration and to ensure that your donation is properly recognized.

Tax Planning: Donating coins can affect your tax situation. Consult a tax professional to understand the tax implications and deductions associated with this donation. This can help you maximize your tax benefits.

Will or Testament: If the deceased expressed specific wishes regarding inherited coins in a will or testament, be sure to honor them in the donation process. Some may have indicated a specific organization or preferred use for the coins.

Transfer of Coins: Once you have completed your assessments, tax planning, and choice of organization, proceed with the transfer of coins. Be sure to follow the specific procedures of the recipient organization. You may need to complete donation and transfer documents.

Recognition and Gratitude: After donating, many charitable organizations recognize your gesture through certificates of recognition. These documents can be useful for tax purposes and testify to your commitment to an important cause.

Family Communication: Involve your family in the donation process. Make sure everyone is aware of your intentions and understands why you have chosen a particular organization or cause.

Promoting Family Legacy: During the donation process, you may want to share the history and legacy associated with the inherited coins. This can add deeper meaning to the donation and the entire numismatic collection.

Perpetuating Numismatic Interest: If your family members still have an interest in numismatics, consider promoting or funding numismatic projects or initiatives in honor of the deceased. This can keep the passion and family legacy alive.

Donating inherited coins to charities or charitable organizations can have a lasting impact on the cause you have chosen to support and, at the same time, preserve the value of your family's numismatic legacy.

Chapter 16: Exploring New Frontiers – Digital Coins and NFTs

From Paper to Bytes: The Advent of Digital Coins

The advent of digital coins has revolutionized the world of numismatics and financial transactions. In this subchapter, we will explore the concept of digital coins, their impact on traditional numismatics, and how you can begin to explore this exciting world.

Digital currencies, also known as cryptocurrencies, are forms of digital currency based on cryptography. The most famous of them are Bitcoin, Ethereum, Ripple, and Litecoin, but the cryptocurrency market is constantly expanding with new coins emerging regularly. Here are some key points to consider:

What is a Cryptocurrency? - A cryptocurrency is a form of digital currency based on blockchain technology, which is a digital record of transactions that cannot be altered. This technology makes cryptocurrencies secure and transparent.

Bitcoin: The Pioneer - Bitcoin was the first cryptocurrency and is still the most famous. It was created in 2009 by an individual or group of individuals under the pseudonym Satoshi Nakamoto. His goal was to create a decentralized digital currency independent of traditional financial institutions.

Ethereum: Smart Contracts - Ethereum is a cryptocurrency that introduced the concept of "smart contracts," which are self-executing programs that facilitate, verify, or implement agreements on blockchain. This has opened up new possibilities for decentralized applications.

Other Cryptocurrencies - In addition to Bitcoin and Ethereum, there are many other cryptocurrencies, each with different characteristics and purposes. Some focus on privacy, others on transaction speed or scalability.

Purchase and Storage - To enter the world of cryptocurrencies, you will first need to purchase some through online exchanges. Once purchased, you will need to store them in a secure digital wallet. There are hardware (physical) and software (application) wallets.

Risk and Regulation - Cryptocurrencies are a high-risk investment, as their prices can be extremely volatile. In addition, regulation of cryptocurrencies varies from country to country and may change over time.

Numismatics and Cryptocurrencies - While cryptocurrencies are a form of digital currency, some people consider them a modern form of numismatics. Digital currencies have intrinsic value based on their usefulness and acceptance in the marketplace.

Investment or Passion - Some people collect cryptocurrencies as part of their passion for technology, while others seek to profit from price fluctuations. It is important to understand your goal when investing in cryptocurrencies.

Security Is Critical - Because cryptocurrencies are vulnerable to hacking and theft, it is essential to take strict security measures to protect your investments.

Cryptocurrencies are a new frontier that offers many opportunities and challenges. If you are interested in exploring this world, it is critical to educate yourself and take precautions to invest responsibly.

The World of NFT: Non-Fungible Tokens and the Future of Coins

In the modern world of digital currencies, a fascinating and revolutionary aspect that is gaining notoriety and popularity are NFTs, which stands for "Non-Fungible Tokens." NFTs represent a unique and indivisible form of digital asset that uses blockchain technology to guarantee ownership and provenance. But what do NFTs actually mean for the world of coins and digital collecting? Let's find out together, going into detail and providing practical examples to guide you through this exciting world.

What Is an NFT?

Let's start with an in-depth explanation. NFTs are digital assets that represent virtual properties or objects. Their distinguishing characteristic is uniqueness and indivisibility. Unlike traditional cryptocurrencies, such as Bitcoin or Ethereum, where each unit is interchangeable with another, NFTs are unique. A practical example would be a limited edition of digital coins, each of which is represented as an NFT, giving each coin a distinct value and rarity. NFTs are registered on a blockchain, an immutable public ledger, which guarantees their authenticity and traceability. In other words, owning an NFT means having digital proof of authenticity and ownership on a decentralized platform.

NFT Applications in Collectibles

One of the most exciting applications of NFTs in the world of coins is the creation of unique digital coins represented as non-fungible tokens. For example, an ancient Roman coin could be digitized as an NFT, with exceptional details that do justice to the original. This NFT could be bought, sold, or traded on specialized platforms. The blockchain ensures that no counterfeit copies can be created, preserving the authenticity of the digital numismatic object. This is just one of the endless possibilities offered by NFTs in the world of collecting. You can also own NFTs of coins from ancient cultures or thematic collections. Diversification of your digital numismatic portfolio is now just a click away.

The Future of Digital Coins

Now that we have explored the definition and applications of NFTs in the world of digital coins, it is time to look to the future. As the technology of NFTs continues to evolve, we may see more and more collectors and investors embracing this form of numismatic activity. You can be one of the pioneers in this new frontier, but remember to do so with care and awareness. As NFTs grow in popularity, it is essential to be informed about market trends, reliable platforms, and potential challenges. Investing in digital currencies through NFTs can offer significant opportunities, but it is important to do research and make thoughtful decisions.

With this subchapter, you will have a solid foundation for understanding the role and potential of NFTs in the world of digital coins. You will be able to assess whether this is a path you wish to pursue in your numismatic collecting and investing journey. Now, we will explore this world further, examining key platforms, best practices, and strategies for maximizing your involvement in the NFT market.

Investing in Digital: Opportunities and Risks

Now that you are familiar with the concept of NFTs and their application in the world of digital coins, it is important to examine the opportunities and risks associated with investing in this rapidly growing sector. NFTs offer new avenues for collecting and investing, but it is critical to make thoughtful and informed decisions. In this subchapter, we will explore the opportunities that NFTs can offer and the potential risks to consider.

NFT Investment Opportunities

Potentially High Yield: Digital coin NFTs have demonstrated significant potential for value appreciation over time. By acquiring unique and rare digital coins, you could benefit from a significant increase in value over the years.

Portfolio Diversification: Investing in digital coins through NFT allows you to diversify your investment portfolio. This can help reduce the overall risk of your portfolio, as digital coins may have a different price correlation than other traditional assets.

Access to Global Collecting: NFTs offer the opportunity to participate in collecting on a global scale. You can own digital coins representing different cultures and eras, thus expanding the scope of your collection.

Risks of NFT Investments

Market Volatility: As with any investment, the NFT market is subject to significant price fluctuations. Digital currencies can experience rapid changes in value, which means you could suffer significant losses.

Fraud and Counterfeiting: The digital nature of NFTs can make it difficult to verify authenticity. It is critical to do thorough research on platforms and sellers to avoid fraud and counterfeiting.

Regulation and Taxes: Regulation of NFTs is still evolving, and taxes associated with digital coin investments can vary by jurisdiction. It is important to be aware of tax implications and local laws.

Competition On: As interest in NFTs increases, competition for acquiring valuable digital coins may be intense. It is possible that it may have to compete with other collectors and investors.

NFT Investment Strategies

To maximize the opportunities and mitigate the risks of digital coin NFT investments, consider adopting a few strategies:

Thorough Research: Before purchasing an NFT, perform comprehensive research on the digital currency and the purchasing platform. Verify the authenticity and reliability of the seller.

Diversification: Don't put all your eggs in one basket. Diversify your NFT portfolio by investing in different digital currencies to reduce risk.

Market Status: Constantly monitor the state of the NFT market. Prices can vary widely, so try to buy when the market is favorable.

Investment Goals: Clearly define your investment goals. Are you looking to collect for passion or to earn a financial return? Your strategies will differ according to your goals.

With a thorough understanding of the opportunities and risks associated with investing in NFTs, you will be able to make informed decisions. In the next subchapter, we will further explore how to integrate digital coins into your physical and virtual collection, making the most of the world of NFTs.

The Virtual Collection: Displaying and Sharing Digital Coins

As you dive into the world of NFTs and digital coins, it is important to consider how you can display and share your virtual collection. Unlike physical coins, digital coins can be displayed and shared online in unique and engaging ways. In this subchapter, we will explore how you can create a virtual showcase for your digital coins and share them with other enthusiasts.

Creating a Virtual Gallery

Visualization Platforms: There are several online platforms that allow you to create customized virtual galleries for your digital coins. These platforms offer options for organizing, labeling, and presenting your coins in an attractive way.

Customization: Take advantage of the customization features to reflect your personality and interests in the virtual storefront. You can select backgrounds, layouts, and styles that fit the theme of your coins.

Detailed Descriptions: Each digital coin should be accompanied by a detailed description explaining its history, authenticity, and key features. This information will enrich the visitor experience.

Sharing and Interaction

Social Media: Use social media to share your digital coins with other collectors. You can post photos, videos, and stories showcasing your collection and start interesting discussions.

Forums and Communities: Participate in online forums and communities of digital coin enthusiasts. These places are great for sharing your discoveries, getting advice, and connecting with like-minded collectors.

Virtual Events: Some virtual events and exhibitions are dedicated exclusively to digital coins and NFTs. Participating in these events can give you an opportunity to showcase your collection to a wider audience.

Exchange and Sale

NFT marketplace: If you are interested in selling or trading your digital coins, explore online marketplaces that specialize in NFTs. Be sure to follow security and authentication procedures when making transactions.

Collection Appreciation: As you show and share your virtual collection, you may discover interest from other collectors. Some may be interested in trading or acquiring your digital coins.

Integration with the Physical Collection

Physical Display: Consider setting aside an area in your homein your home dedicated to your physical and digital coin collection. You can use screens and devices to display digital coins in a physical environment.

Multimedia Links: Create links between physical coins and corresponding digital versions. For example, you might have a QR code linked to a digital coin that represents the physical one.

Synergy Between Physical and Digital Coins: Explore how the two forms of collecting can enrich each other. For example, you might look for physical coins linked to specific digital coins.

As you dive deeper and deeper into the world of digital coins and NFTs, remember that sharing and interaction can greatly enrich your collecting experience. In the next subchapter, we will examine how to integrate digital coins into your physical collection, creating a link between the virtual and real worlds.

The Integration of Digital Coins into the Physical Collection

As you delve into the fascinating world of digital coins and NFTs, you may wonder how they can be integrated into your physical coin collection. In this subchapter, we will explore different strategies for connecting digital coins to your real collection, creating a meaningful link between the two worlds.

1. Physical and Virtual Association

One of the first strategies is to physically associate digital coins with the tangible collection. You can do this in several ways:

QR Code and NFC: Applies QR codes or NFC (Near Field Communication) devices to physical coins. By scanning the code or approaching an NFC device, visitors can access the corresponding digital coins and online information.

Descriptive Labels: Create descriptive labels or tags for your physical coins that also include information about the digital versions. This will allow visitors to further explore the online collection.

2. Digital Twinning

The concept of "digital twinning" involves creating an exact digital version of a physical object. In the context of digital coins and physical collections, you can adopt this strategy in the following way:

Digital Asset Creation: For each physical coin, create a corresponding digital asset in the form of an NFT. This asset should be an exact replica of the physical coin, complete with high-resolution images and detailed information.

Tokenization: Use an NFT platform to tokenize digital assets. Each physical coin will have its corresponding token, which can be purchased, traded, or collected by others.

Bidirectional Linking: Make sure that NFT tokens are bidirectionally linked to physical coins. This way, anyone who owns a physical coin can access the corresponding digital asset and vice versa.

3. Advanced Visualization

In the digital world, you have access to advanced visualization tools that can enhance the experience of your digital and physical coins:

3D models: Use 3D models of the coins to allow visitors to explore every detail interactively.

Virtual reality (VR): If you have access to VR technology, create immersive experiences where digital and physical coins can be explored in a virtual environment.

Augmented reality (AR): Leverage AR apps to offer interactive information when visitors point their devices at physical coins or images of them.

4. Physical and Virtual Exposure

If you have a space dedicated to your physical coins, consider integrating digital coins into the display as well:

Interactive Screens: Place interactive screens near the physical coins where visitors can explore the corresponding digital coins.

Multimedia Presentations: Organize multimedia presentations that include physical and digital coins, providing an engaging and informative experience.

Virtual Visits: Allow online visitors to participate in virtual tours of your collection, where they can explore both physical and digital coins.

Integrating digital coins into your physical collection adds an innovative and engaging element to your collecting. In the next subchapter, we will examine the synergies between the two forms of collecting and how they can enrich each other.

Chapter 17: Ten of the World's Most Famous Coin Collections

The Collection of Queen Elizabeth II

One of the most prestigious coin collections in the world is that of Her Majesty Queen Elizabeth II of the United Kingdom. This extraordinary numismatic collection is the result of a hereditary passion for numismatics that has lasted for generations in the British royal family.

Origin of the Collection: Queen Elizabeth II's collection began with her grandfather, King George V, who had a passion for numismatics and coin art. Over time, the collection was expanded and enriched by other members of the royal family, including Elizabeth II's father, King George VI.

An Eclectic Collection: The collection includes a wide range of coins, from ancient Roman and Greek coins to medieval and modern coins. It is notable for its eclecticism and variety of coins from different eras and regions of the world. Each coin is carefully selected for its historical, artistic, or numismatic value.

The Queen Collector: Queen Elizabeth II herself was an avid coin collector and contributed significantly to the expansion and care of the collection. She was known to be personally involved in the selection of coins to acquire and was well informed about numismatics.

Public Exhibition: Queen Elizabeth II's collection is often displayed to the public in various exhibitions, thus helping to educate the public about the world of coins and history. It is a testament to the cultural and historical importance of coins and the British royal family's passion for numismatics.

The Smithsonian Institution Collection

The Smithsonian Institution, based in Washington, D.C., is one of the most prestigious museum institutions in the world and houses one of the most significant and diverse numismatic collections. Founded in 1846, the Smithsonian has become a landmark for the preservation and display of coins.

A National Treasure: The Smithsonian's numismatic collection has thousands of coins from every corner of the world. What makes it unique is its diversity, with coins spanning millennia of human history. One can find ancient coins from Ancient Greece and Rome, medieval coins, American colonial coins, and much more.

Expansion Continues: The Smithsonian continues to expand its collection through acquisitions and donations. The Smithsonian's numismatic experts work tirelessly to identify and acquire coins of historical and artistic significance. This ongoing effort has made the collection one of the most comprehensive and diverse in the world.

An Educational Resource: In addition to the coin exhibit, the Smithsonian offers a wide range of educational resources for the public. These resources include publications, educational programs, traveling exhibitions, and even a conservation laboratory dedicated to coins. This allows the public to learn in depth about numismatic history.

A Historical Legacy: The Smithsonian's numismatic collection is more than just a coin display. It represents a significant part of humanity's financial, cultural, and economic history. Its preservation and public access to this numismatic legacy are essential to the understanding of our past and present.

Stack's Bowers Galleries Collection

Stack's Bowers Galleries is one of the world's most renowned numismatic auction houses and manages an extraordinary collection of coins, tokens, and banknotes. Founded in 1933, this auction house has a long history of numismatic expertise and has held some of the most significant auction sales in the history of coins.

A Heritage of Exceptional Sales: Stack's Bowers Galleries is famous for its auction sales of rare and valuable coins. It has sold some of the rarest and most expensive numismatic pieces in the world, setting price records in several categories. These sales have attracted global attention and made the auction house a destination for collectors and investors.

World-Class Numismatic Expertise: The experts at Stack's Bowers Galleries are renowned for their coin knowledge and appraisal skills. They have helped identify and authenticate many of the rarest and most important coins, ensuring the confidence of collectors and investors.

An Evolving Collection: The Stack's Bowers Galleries collection is constantly evolving due to new acquisitions made through the auctions they regularly hold. This means that the collection reflects numismatic market trends and offers a unique view of the most interesting and valuable coins available.

An Opportunity for Collectors: Although many of the pieces in Stack's Bowers Galleries collection are sold through public auctions, this presents an opportunity for collectors worldwide. Auctions offer the chance to purchase rare and valuable coins, helping to spread the passion for numismatics.

Preserving the Numismatic Past: Stack's Bowers Galleries is not only a place to buy and sell rare coins, but also a custodian of the numismatic past. Their focus on coin preservation and documentation helps preserve numismatic heritage for future generations.

The Louvre's Collection of Ancient Coins

The Louvre, one of the world's most famous museums, houses an extraordinary collection of ancient coins spanning a wide range of eras and cultures. This collection represents tangible evidence of past civilizations and offers a unique opportunity to explore history through coins.

The Louvre—A Must-Stop for Collectors: The Louvre Museum in Paris is a mecca for art and history enthusiasts. Its collection of ancient coins is considered one of the most important in the world and is a must-see for collectors and numismatic scholars.

Coins from Antiquity to the Middle Ages: The Louvre's collection covers a vast historical period, from the coins of ancient Greece and Rome to those of the European Middle Ages. This variety provides a comprehensive overview of the evolution of coinage over the centuries.

Treasures of Art and History: Many of the coins on display at the Louvre are not just numismatic objects, but authentic works of art. Many of them feature exceptional artistic details, including depictions of deities, emperors, and historical events. Exploring this collection is an experience that combines art and history in a unique way.

A Bridge Between Cultures: The Louvre collection also bears witness to the encounter and exchange between different cultures through coinage. The coins of ancient empires often circulated far beyond their borders, creating a bridge between distant civilizations.

Coins as Historical Documents: Ancient coins are true historical sources. They bear inscriptions, symbols, and representations that tell stories of conquests, trade, and daily life in ages past. Studying these coins is a fascinating way to explore history from a unique perspective.

An Ode to Preservation: The Louvre devotes great attention to the preservation of its ancient coins. This commitment ensures that these precious pieces are preserved for future generations of collectors, scholars, and history buffs.

Collectors and the Louvre: Many people who visit the Louvre are inspired by its collection of ancient coins and decide to embark on their own collecting journey. This collection not only offers a window into history, but can also influence new enthusiasts to start their own numismatic collections.

The Louvre's collection of ancient coins is a true testament to the historical and artistic richness that coins can represent. Exploring it is a journey through time and the civilizations that left their mark on world history.

The Dubai Emirate Coin Collection

The Emirate of Dubai is known for its extraordinary wealth and commitment to preserving history through coin collecting. Its numismatic collection is a treasure trove of precious coins and is a fascinating exploration of the cultures and eras that helped shape the region.

The Emirate's Rich Heritage: The Emirate of Dubai has invested considerable resources in the creation and care of its coin collection. This commitment is evident in the thousands of coins, ancient and modern, that make up the collection.

A Phenomenal Numismatic Diversity: The Emirate of Dubai's collection embraces a wide diversity of coins, covering eras from antiquity to the present day. Here, you can find coins from ancient Mesopotamia, medieval Islamic coins, and even more recent coins issued after the founding of the United Arab Emirates.

Gold and Silver Coins: Among the most precious gems in this collection are the gold and silver coins that reflect the luxury and wealth of Dubai. These precious metals were often used to mint coins of great value.

The Combination of Art and History: As in many other coin collections, art plays an important role. Many coins feature elaborate designs, decorative calligraphy, and cultural symbols. These coins represent a fascinating marriage of art and history.

An Expression of Cultural Identity: Dubai's coin collection also reflects the emirate's cultural identity and its history of trade, growth, and prosperity. These coins are testimony to the cultural and commercial influences that have shaped the region over the centuries.

Commitment to the Future: The Emirate of Dubai is not only dedicated to preserving the coins of the past, but also to creating new commemorative and numismatic coins that celebrate significant events and personalities. This tradition is a sign of commitment to the future of numismatics.

A Source of Inspiration: The Emirate of Dubai's coin collection is not only a treasure trove of historical and financial value, but also a source of inspiration for collectors and enthusiasts around the world. This collection demonstrates how coin collecting can be an art form, an investment, and a testament to history and cultural identity.

Exploring the Emirate of Dubai's coin collection is a journey through time and culture, and it is an incredible example of how coins can be treasures that connect the past, present, and future.

The Singapore Numismatic Collection

Singapore's numismatic collection is an exceptional treasure trove of coins that reflects the rich and varied history of this multicultural and cosmopolitan nation. Through a wide range of coins, it tells the story of the island from its colonial roots to modernity.

Colonial Roots: The collection begins with coins dating back to colonial times, when Singapore was part of the British Empire. Coins from this period often feature British symbols and coats of arms, as well as representing the early impact of colonialism on the region.

The Era of Independence: With independence achieved in 1965, Singapore began minting its own coins. This period is represented in the collection with coins that celebrate the national identity and pride of the emerging nation.

Singapore's Cultural Diversity: Singapore's ethnic diversity is evident in its coin collection. Coins from different cultures such as Chinese, Malaysian, Indian, and Peranakan are part of the collection, reflecting Singapore's multicultural identity.

Commemorative Coins: The collection features a variety of commemorative coins issued to celebrate significant events, charismatic leaders, or national milestones. These coins often represent cultural icons or national symbols, emphasizing national pride and unity.

Union and Progress: The collection also reflects Singapore's commitment to unity and progress through coins that symbolize the cohesion between different ethnic groups and religions that peacefully coexist in this nation.

Technological Innovation: Singapore is known for its constant innovation and technological advancement. The collection includes coins that incorporate advanced minting technologies and modern designs, demonstrating a desire to keep up with the times.

Numismatic Education: Singapore's collection is also an educational tool, helping to spread historical and cultural awareness through exhibitions and educational programs. This commitment to education helps to preserve and promote numismatic culture.

Exploring Singapore's numismatic collection is a journey through the history, culture, and identity of this dynamic nation. The coins collected represent a tangible record of Singapore's journey from its colonial roots to the modern city-state.

The Collection of the Egyptian Museum in Cairo

The Egyptian Museum in Cairo is world famous for its outstanding collection of artifacts and, of course, coins, which form a significant part of its exhibition. This collection offers a valuable window into the history of ancient Egypt through the prism of coins, revealing surprising aspects of ancient Egyptian civilization.

Coins As Historical Documents: The Egyptian Museum's collection contains a wide range of coins, many of which date back to ancient Egypt. These coins are like miniature historical documents, recording events, dynasties, and leaders of the time.

World's Oldest Coin: One of the gems of the collection is the famous gold coin of Nekhthorheb, which dates back to 350 B.C.E. It is one of the oldest coins in the world and is an outstanding example of the skill of Egyptian coinmakers.

Coins of the Pharaohs: The collection includes a number of coins issued by various pharaohs that provide unique details about their lives and ruling dynasties. These coins often show Egyptian gods, symbols of power, and hieroglyphics that tell the story.

Coins As Objects of Worship: Many objects in the museum demonstrate how coins were used in religious rituals and as funerary offerings in the tombs of the ancient Egyptians. This gives us an idea of their spiritual importance.

The Roman Period: The collection also extends to the period when Egypt was part of the Roman Empire. Coins from this period often depict Roman emperors and demonstrate the Roman cultural influence on Egyptian monetary art.

Coins As Means of Exchange: In addition to their historical and religious value, ancient Egyptian coins give us insight into what daily life was like and how people related to money in the ancient Egyptian world.

The Mystery of Ancient Egypt: The Egyptian Museum's collection is an invitation to explore the mystery and intrigue of ancient Egypt through the filter of coins. The coins offer a tangible way to connect with the art, culture, and history of this extraordinary civilization.

Special Exhibitions: The museum often organizes special exhibitions devoted to its coins, highlighting exceptional pieces and offering visitors a unique opportunity to deepen their understanding of ancient Egypt.

The numismatic collection of the Egyptian Museum in Cairo is an extraordinary testimony to ancient Egyptian civilization and an important piece in the puzzle of world history. The collected coins are not only objects of historical value, but also doors that allow us to enter the fascinating and enigmatic world of ancient Egypt.

The Coin Collection of the State Hermitage Museum

The State Hermitage Museum in St. Petersburg, Russia, is renowned for its outstanding art collection, which also includes a large and impressive coin collection. This collection is a hidden gem within the museum's walls and offers a fascinating perspective on the history of numismatics and art in Russia and around the world.

A Journey Through Russian Numismatics: The Hermitage Museum's coin collection offers a comprehensive overview of the history of Russian numismatics, from the coins of local pre-Russian tribes to the coins of the Russian Empire to the coins of the Soviet era and beyond. This journey through time is fascinating and provides a complete picture of Russia's economic and political development.

Numismatic Treasures of the Russian Empire: Among the most impressive pieces in the collection are the coins of the Russian Empire, with their elaborate designs and finely crafted details. The gold coins of the tsars, such as those of Catherine the Great and Nicholas II, are particularly fascinating.

The Art of the Mint: The collection demonstrates the skill of Russian coin makers in creating miniature works of art. Hermitage coins are often decorated with intricate details, artistic depictions, and Cyrillic texts that add an aesthetic element to the monetary value.

A Window to the World: The Hermitage Museum's collection is not limited to Russian coins; it also includes coins from around the world. This diversity reflects Russia's global connections through trade and diplomacy and offers a broader view of numismatic history.

Coins As Political Tools: The Hermitage coins tell stories of power and politics, reflecting Russia's social and political transformations over the centuries. Many coins commemorate historical events, regime changes, and important leaders.

Special Exhibitions: The State Hermitage Museum regularly holds special exhibitions devoted to its coins, which enable visitors to deepen their understanding of Russian numismatics and history.

The Legacy of Peter the Great: Much of the collection was assembled by Peter the Great, the tsar who opened Russia to Western Europe in the 18th century. His passion for numismatics laid the foundation for this exceptional collection.

An Educational Experience: Visiting the Hermitage Museum's coin collection is an educational experience, as it offers not only a perspective on monetary history, but also on the artistic and cultural influences that have shaped Russia and the world.

The State Hermitage Museum's coin collection is a unique and valuable legacy that reflects the complex and fascinating history of Russia and humanity itself through the prism of numismatics. Exploring these coins is an extraordinary way to travel back in time and better understand the influences that shaped the modern world.

The Numismatic Collection of the British Museum

The British Museum in London is one of the most famous museums in the world, known for its vast collection of global art and culture. Within its walls is an exceptional numismatic collection, spanning millennia of history and culture through coins.

Ancient Origins: The British Museum's numismatic collection has deep roots in history. It was founded in 1753, when numismatic collector and scholar Sir Hans Sloane donated his personal collection to the state, forming the nucleus of the collection. This gesture laid the foundation for one of the most significant numismatic collections in the world.

A Global Collection: The British Museum's collection spans a wide range of cultures and civilizations. It includes coins from ancient Greece and Rome, medieval Europe, Asia, Africa, and many other parts of the world. This diversity reflects the broad scope of human history.

The Art of Coins: Many of the coins in the British Museum's collection are miniature works of art. Ancient coins often feature elaborate designs, cultural symbols, and portraits of rulers. They skillfully combine economic function and artistic expression.

An Integration with History and Culture: The British Museum's numismatic collection is not just a collection of coins, but a window into history and culture. Coins are often used to explore the political, social, and economic changes of past civilizations.

Iconic Coins: Among the most famous coins are the Athenian coins of the fifth century B.C.E., the talents of Rhodes, the Roman coins with the effigy of Julius Caesar, and the gold coins of the Kingdom of Macedonia. Each of these coins tells a unique story.

A Hub for Numismatic Research: The British Museum is a major center for numismatic research. Scholars and coin experts from around the world come here to study the collection and conduct in-depth research on global monetary history.

Exhibitions and Educational Programs: The museum organizes special exhibitions and educational programs that provide opportunities for the public to deepen their understanding of coins and related history. These initiatives make numismatics accessible to a wider audience.

Global Impact: The British Museum's collection has a global impact, contributing to the understanding of human history and the sharing of knowledge through traveling exhibitions and international collaborations.

The British Museum's numismatic collection is an invaluable resource for numismatic enthusiasts, scholars, and audiences interested in world history and culture. It offers a unique opportunity to explore global connections through the art of coins and to immerse oneself in stories thousands of years old.

The Coin Collection of the Beijing Institute of Numismatics

The Beijing Numismatic Institute, as the "Beijing Numismatic Institute," houses one of the most significant and indispensable numismatic collections in Asia and the world. This facility is a landmark for coin enthusiasts and numismatic scholars, offering a broad overview of Chinese monetary history and beyond.

A Millennial History: The collection of the Beijing Institute of Numismatics reflects a numismatic history spanning millennia. It includes coins from the earliest Chinese forms of exchange to the imperial coins of the Qing Dynasty and modern republican coins. This wide range of numismatic eras provides a window into China's economic and political development through the centuries.

The Art of Chinese Coins: Chinese coins are famous for their artistic features. Imperial coins often feature finely elaborate details, iconic designs, and elegant lettering. Coins from the Beijing Institute of Numismatics display this artistry in all its magnificence.

Coins of Cultural Value: Many Chinese coins have deep cultural and historical value. For example, sword coins, ancient coins with central holes, were often worn as amulets or auspicious symbols. These coins testify to ancient beliefs and traditions.

A Bridge to Global Understanding: The Chinese Numismatic Collection is not limited to Chinese coins. It also includes foreign coins that have been in circulation in China through ancient trade routes, showing the global connections of this region.

Research and Education: The Beijing Institute of Numismatics is a leading research center in China and around the world. Scholars travel here to study Chinese coins and to collaborate on numismatic research. The institute also offers educational programs to bring the public closer to numismatics and Chinese monetary history.

A National Treasure: The collection of the Beijing Institute of Numismatics is considered a national treasure and cultural heritage of China. It is a place where history, art, and culture come together through the medium of coins.

Exhibitions and Special Events: The institute regularly hosts exhibitions and special events to share its numismatic riches with the public. These exhibitions are an opportunity to see some of the world's rarest and most fascinating coins.

The numismatic collection of the Beijing Institute of Numismatics is a testament to China's rich numismatic heritage and offers a valuable window into the history and culture of this region. Numismatic enthusiasts and scholars will find this collection an invaluable resource for deepening their understanding of Chinese and global monetary history.

Conclusions: The Numismatic Journey Continues

In this compelling exploration of the world of coins, we have traveled through time and space, discovering the extraordinary diversity and richness of numismatics. Along our journey, you have absorbed a wide range of knowledge, tools, and strategies that have transformed you into an informed collector and investor.

We started with the basics, building your arsenal of tools and knowledge to approach the world of coins with confidence. From ancient coins to modern coins, you learned how to analyze the characteristics that define the value and uniqueness of each coin.

The digital world has no secrets for you now: you have discovered online resources that can enhance your numismatic experience, enabling you to search, learn, and connect with other enthusiasts around the world.

We also explored the delicate process of coin preservation, ensuring that your collection remains in optimal condition for generations to come. And investment strategies have provided you with opportunities to grow the value of your collection over time.

But not everything took place without challenges. We faced the threat of counterfeit coins, carefully examining the characteristics that distinguish the real from the fake. In addition, you learned how to protect your collection and the actions you can take to reduce risk.

Finally, our numismatic journey has no boundaries. Your passion for coins is endless, and your numismatic discoveries and adventures are bound to continue. Whether you are a novice or a veteran collector, your coins tell stories, depict history, and represent your connection to a numismatic heritage that spans centuries.

So as we conclude this phase of our journey, remember that the world of coins is a place of endless discovery. Continue to explore, collect, and share this wonderful passion with the world. Your coins are a personal treasure, but also a bridge between the past, present, and future.

Wear your numismatist's hat proudly and get ready for your next adventures. Our numismatic journey is eternal, as is your passion. Bon voyage, dear collector!

Glossary

Alloy: The metal composition of a coin—for example, whether it is gold, silver, or copper.

Basic Arsenal: A set of essential tools for coin collectors, including magnifying glass, scales, caliper, and numismatic catalog.

Choice: A coin that has been selected for its superior quality and condition.

Circulation: The total number of copies of a particular coin minted.

Date of Issue: The date on which a coin was minted.

Denomination: The face value of a currency, often expressed in terms of monetary units such as dollars, euros, or pounds.

Diameter: The measure of the width of a coin, often expressed in millimeters.

Edge: The outer edge of a coin.

FDC (Brilliant Uncirculated): The highest quality of condition for a coin, with no signs of wear.

Gold Bars: Solid bars of gold that represent a type of investment in precious metals.

Issuance: The production of coins by a mint or monetary authority.

Magnifying Glass: An instrument that allows close observation and identification of details on a coin.

Mint: An institution authorized to mint coins.

Mint Mark: A symbol or letter stamped on a coin to indicate the mint where it was struck.

Numismatic Appraiser: An expert who appraises coins and determines their value.

Numismatic Catalog: A publication that lists and describes coins in circulation or collectibles, often with estimated values.

Numismatic Certificate: An official document issued by a numismatic authority attesting to the authenticity and condition of a coin.

Numismatic Collection: A collection of coins obtained by an individual for purposes of interest, passion, or investment.

Numismatic Grade: The condition rating of a coin, usually on a scale from "P" (Poor) to "FDC" (Fleur-de-Coin, or Brilliant Uncirculated).

Numismatic Grade (Extended): A detailed assessment of a coin's condition, often with subcategories such as "splendid" or "excellent."

Numismatic Investment: The purchase of coins with the goal of making a profit in the future.

Numismatic Passion: The deep affection and interest in numismatics and coins.

Numismatics: The study and collection of coins and banknotes.

Numismatic Scales: A precision instrument used by collectors to weigh their coins.

Paper Money: A form of currency consisting of paper bills instead of metal coins.

Patina: The layer of oxidation or discoloration that forms on the surface of a coin over time.

Quality Proof: Specially minted coins with superior finishes, often collected for their beauty and impeccable condition.

Rarity: The degree of scarcity or frequency with which a particular coin appears on the market.

Recognizing Counterfeits: The ability to identify counterfeit versus genuine coins.

Special Issue: A limited series of coins issued with a unique feature or in honor of a special event.

Storage Guide: A set of methods and tips for storing coins safely and avoiding damage.

Time Zone: The division of the world into distinct standard times based on latitude, which is important for the calculation of coin issue dates.

Valuation: The process of determining the approximate value of a coin.

Vintage: The year in which a coin was minted.

Wear: The erosion and abrasion that a coin undergoes with use and the passage of time.

Made in the USA
Las Vegas, NV
19 February 2024

86000488R00059